Joy in t

Marjorie Idle

First published 1988

Cover photo: John Lacey

British Library Cataloguing in Publication Data
Idle, Marjorie
Joy in the city.
1. Church of England. Clergy. Wives.
Christian life. Biographies
I. Title
248.4'830435

ISBN 0–86065–565–2

First edition published by Kingsway Publications.
This edition printed for
David Poyser, North Street, Reading RG7 5EX by
The Cromwell Press, Melksham, Wiltshire SN12 8PH

To Christopher and the boys, many of whom ate their shredded wheat over my fair copy

Contents

Foreword

by Bishop Jim Thompson

It would be impossible for me to be objective about *Joy in the City*. Every page is a picture gallery of East London and Limehouse in particular — of its beauty and ugliness. The heroes are the people — from China, Bangladesh, Poplar, Limehouse, Stepney, the West Indies and the rest of the world — Christians, Muslims, Hindus. In spite of the arson and the vandalism, the disappointments and set-backs, Marjorie Idle breathes optimism and faith through these pages.

I am delighted that the wife of one of our East London vicars has found the space to write a book. Although Marjorie is very much a person in her own right, she is also totally involved in her husband Chris's work. She lives her life under God and sees the signs of his activity and his love all around her — whether it be in the sunset over the canal, or the baking, or the new achievements of her recorder pupils. I was constantly reminded of the hymn 'Teach me, my God and King, in all things Thee to see'. For some this might seem too simple, but the book carries the conviction that the writer travels closely with God and so discovers joy where others despair.

It's a book that made me laugh and yet there are inevitable sadnesses. It is a commonplace story, but one which is run through with light and hope. What transforms the ordinary into the extraordinary, and converts the mundane into the other worldly, is the love of Christ and the faith that in his hands somehow all will be well. Since *Faith in the City* many people have asked me what the inner city is like — they could do a lot worse than read this vivid description of the life of a mum, a teacher, a wife in Limehouse and taste the joy in it.

Jim Thompson

Preface

A good deal of water has flowed down the Thames since the first edition of this book in 1988. We have worked in Suffolk for nearly seven years, and are now about to make our home in the inner city again.

The deserted wharf we knew, where boats from the Canary Islands had ceased to unload their wealth, now supports the highest tower block in Europe — the Canary Wharf development.

But this book is still historically true, and still conveys the flavour of Limehouse.

May God bless John and Angela Pearce, who succeeded us, their parishoners and their successors.

Marjorie Idle
Oakley, Suffolk 1995

I

Here, in the city

Lord, thou hast been our refuge from one generation to another.
Before the mountains were brought forth, or ever the earth and the world were made, thou art God from everlasting and world without end (Ps 90:1, 2).

The signal turned green and the train picked up speed, heading through Bermondsey towards London Bridge. I turned to the window, gazing north across the river for a glimpse of the huge church that Hawksmoor built in Limehouse.

You would think we had been away for years, the way we always look out for the church tower. Today I had only been a few miles but I leaned against the window as eager as ever to see a sight I had seen from the bedroom window only this morning.

Suddenly I was surprised. After all these years living close to the church I thought I had seen it in every setting. This afternoon the bright spring sun was nearly on the horizon. Behind the church and the tower blocks of East London there were storm clouds banked, charcoal and indigo; and against this dramatic back-cloth the whole skyline stood clear in the sunlight, black and white and gold. Just for a few moments it had become fairyland.

The guard handed down my bicycle at London Bridge and said, 'Could do with a coat of paint, couldn't 'e?'

I shook my head.

'Not while I live in London,' I said. 'This way it looks too tatty for anyone to steal it.'

Ten minutes later I was cycling past the Tower of London, leaving the old Royal Mint on the left and Tower Bridge on the right, into the Highway and homewards. Slowly after Dock Street, toiling a bit up the slope. I'm not one of your keen cyclists, coming home in teeming rain to drip all over the kitchen. I merely potter along on fine days, saving bus fares and time.

Past the Strangers' Rest now, a handsome new building for a veteran mission work. Sixty years ago my parents, newly engaged, came over from South Norwood from time to time to help with the services in the old Mission building. My mother played the harmonium. Never dreaming that the bombing would obliterate the old Ratcliffe Highway. Never dreaming their daughter would cycle along a wide new road simply called The Highway.

When I was ten we went to stay with friends and there on the bookshelf, among the absolutely topping schoolgirl stories and a row of books by Amy LeFeuvre, whose nice children grew up in Edwardian nurseries, was a book that held me spellbound. I thought I was reading it secretly, until my father found me one day and took it away as I knew he would. It was not suitable for me, he said.

But the damage was done. The trumpet call had sounded. The book was *God in the slums* by Hugh Redwood. How interesting, I thought, that some of the people of East London should 'pour torrents of abuse' upon ministers of the Gospel; I wondered if that would ever happen to me. It hasn't. Even more interesting was that an irate woman poured the contents of a full chamberpot upon the head of a man of God. I haven't seen that happen either. Not yet.

And so, subconsciously for most of the time, I spent my schooldays and my years of nursing waiting for the time when I too would come to East London.

Cycling along this March afternoon, I came to the junction with Butcher Row, near the Royal Foundation of St. Katharine. I slid off the saddle and walked across the road at the lights, too scared to make a right-hand turn in the face of such fierce and fast opposition from the other traffic.

Suddenly it was quiet. The canal bridge in Narrow Street was under repair, so all the traffic had turned left up to the main road. On the right were old warehouses, beautifully restored and made into riverside flats. On the left, more warehouses, awaiting an unknown fate.

The bridge was blocked off with red and white cones; and there, across the canal, was our parish—Limehouse. The sunlight glinted on the water in the Regent's Canal Dock; the quayside was empty and lifeless but greatly coveted by the property developers. They want to build waterside houses for the rich; they are opposed by the Limehouse Development Group who want the space used for homes and recreation for the people of the borough. Meanwhile the anglers have it to themselves.

The property of the Port of London Authority is carefully guarded even in these slack times, so I said a polite 'Good afternoon' to a man watching as I carried my bicycle down the steps to the lockside. I wheeled it across the top of the lock-gates, gritted my teeth and tried not to look down when I came to the angle where the gates meet.

The storm clouds which had seemed so threatening from the train window had now disappeared and Narrow Street ahead of me was a contrast. Deep shadows thrown by Hough's Paper Mills and pale sunlight on the roofs of the riverside houses—Doctor David Owen's, an old pub called 'The Grapes', and lodging for members of the Diplomatic Service. I turned into Northey Street, past the short row of houses that were occupied when we first came. I had fancied one of them—nice little cottages they were. Now they are empty and falling to pieces. At the bend is the old Harbour Master's house; it must have been pleasant living there, looking out over the busy traffic in the Basin. But this too is now derelict. The whole of this once-busy street is in ruins. The river traffic has moved to Tilbury, down river, where it is easier to deal with containers.

I cycled carefully, avoiding the potholes and rubbish and turned into Oak Lane. You go along between a high concrete wall on one side and corrugated iron on the other, and there comes a place just a few yards long where you can see nothing except the narrow road and its grey boundaries. Even on a bicycle on a sunny day I dread it. Then suddenly the tower blocks and new flats are ahead, and the church tower.

Turn left up our street under the railway bridge and you begin to hear the incessant roar of the traffic in Commercial Road. Two boys on their way home from school nodded and said,

'Hi, Mrs Idle.' Grown so tall. When they were at junior school I taught them to play the recorder.

Up the slope past the old houses and there in our garden, flung against the afternoon sky, was a flowering cherry tree in full bloom. New life and hope amidst the greyness. There is hope for Limehouse because God is at work. He has not moved down-river.

People often say to me, 'What is it like, living in Limehouse?' All I can do is talk about life as I find it and the people who are my friends. I fell into step with President Mugabe on the zebra crossing one day. (Not the real one; just his look-alike.)

'No stick today?' I asked. He gave me one of his warm smiles.

'Well, you have to try, don't you? If I go far from home or have to take a bus, then I bring my stick with me.' I walked slowly beside him while he took each careful step, his left arm stiff across his chest.

'Don't you feel safer when you've got your stick?' I persisted.

'Oh no, it's not the stick, it's people. Last week on this crossing a driver shouted out to me, "Go home you dirty black." But in the very same week. . . .' His gravelly West African voice thickened and his tribal scars moved up to meet his lower eyelids as he smiled at the memory—'in the very same week, a driver got out of his cab, got down and helped me across the road. It's people every time. People.'

It would be difficult to find a more cosmopolitan mix of people anywhere. Sherlock Holmes used to come here, seeking his quarry in some opium den while the thick reeking fog drifted up from the river. We have no fogs now, nor opium dens that we know of, but Chinatown still stretches north and east of the church—smart restaurants where you have to book and a handful of friendly take-aways.

They are still reprinting an old Gospel chorus that goes —

'Jesus loves the wee Chinese
Far away across the seas. . . .'

When our boys first heard it they fell about laughing; had the author never been to Limehouse? In every school there are friendly bilingual Chinese children at the top of the chess championship; in every take-away they tot up your bill in English and chat in Cantonese.

Our main cluster of shops is in Salmon Lane, just opposite. Rose and George on the greengrocery stall, big Roger in the butcher's and Irene with her lovely smile in the baker's. The dry cleaners are Italians. Then there's Lou's Fish Bar, run by Chinese since Lou and his great fat cat retired, Cherie's Cafe, the Golden Tandoori, the Local Friends, the Canton and the Good Friends. Good gracious, do we eat all that much in Limehouse?

The Local Friends is run by a tiny little old man and his wife. He busies himself among the woks on the gas-range while she writes the order for your take-away. Then they confer in a language so Oriental that you expect to hear a Chinese gong sounding at any moment. More smiles, a shaking and hissing of woks and soon your sweetcorn soup is ready.

Down at the Good Friends restaurant everything is sophisticated, with a pleasant blend of western furnishing and eastern cooking. Pink tablecloths, puce chairs, and it's nice when your friends take you there and foot the bill.

Round the corner is Chinatown restaurant and across the road is On's Take-away.

'My mother,' read David at the school Harvest Festival one year, 'is a very good cook. She can cook all of the fifty-five items on our menu.' I second that. It is our favourite place for buying a celebration meal.

Next to On's used to be Chung's store. I still miss it but as old Mr Chung looked about a hundred, I don't begrudge him his retirement. I bought rice in there, four pounds at a time. Mr Chung dibbed it out of a sack on the floor with an old baked bean tin. If I bought noodles as well, or perhaps a tin of lychees for a treat, he would add up the bill on his abacus. Then we would smile formally and he would bow as he handed me my change. And when I used the rice I would try to remember to wash it.

Beyond are Ming Street and Canton Street and Pennyfields.

'Ah, there was a time when you walked up Pennyfields and never saw a western face.' So for those who so often ask 'Is Limehouse still the Chinese quarter?' the answer is Yes.

Which does not tie up neatly the population around here. Ever since the Anglo-Saxons invaded Stebonhay, now Stepney, there have been visitors who stayed on. The most famous were the Huguenots who came to

Spitalfields and the Jews who came to Whitechapel. And to Limehouse, as elsewhere, have come Indians and West Indians, Pakistanis and Bengalis—and more recently Vietnamese.

Ann came into the school staffroom with very bright eyes one morning and I did not know at first what the brightness was.

'Did you have a good cooking group?' I asked as we fetched our coffee.

'Oh, they loved it,' she said. 'Some of them relaxed and started chatting in a way they haven't before. Quy said she remembered swimming in the sea with her father. He was swimming using only his legs to push him along.' Ann rubbed a hand across her eyes which had suddenly become too bright.

'Even then I didn't cotton on to what Quy was talking about. So I said, "Why wasn't your Daddy using his arms to swim?" and she said, "Well, he was holding me and my little brother up". We are not a sentimental lot, in our staffroom, but we were all caught up for a moment in the vivid picture of escaping 'boat people' and Molly said, 'Quy was one of the lucky ones, wasn't she? Must have been terrible, all those that drowned on the way.'

But now the Vietnamese too have become part of the rich mixture that is Limehouse.

When I started teaching at Cyril Jackson School, in 1978, half the children were non-English mother tongue, but now that figure is 70%. Madeline Fong comes in to teach the Chinese children both in their own language and in English, and Sheila does the same for the Bengalis. The letters ESL—English as a second language—have become part of my vocabulary.

Going to church on holiday is always slightly strange. I look around the congregation in Tonbridge or Southsea or wherever and think for a hideous, homesick moment, 'Help, this isn't a proper church, they're all white.'

It is in this rich mixture of society that our family has grown up. My husband is Christopher Idle, rector of

Limehouse. Our sons are dispersed far and wide—Timothy in Alabama, Jonathan studying in Birmingham and Jeremy in Edinburgh. Marcus is still at home, working his way through the sixth form.

They came to Limehouse as juniors and have shared the joys and sorrows with us over these ten years. We live in a gracious modern rectory, built before the squeeze on finance, and replacing the huge eighteenth century building across the road that fell apart with dry rot.

Behind the house, beyond the garden wall, is the church. Hawksmoor put it up, Hitler failed to knock it down. It stands as a symbol of hope, even for those who do not know it is God they are looking for.

2

Magnificent

I was glad when they said unto me 'We will go into the house of the Lord' (Ps 122:1).

In spring, a young architect's fancy lightly turns to thoughts of Limehouse. He makes a tour of the Hawksmoor churches, beginning with Christ Church Spitalfields. This noble building has been made safe in the last ten years and is now used for worship and for concerts after years of closure.

Next comes St George-in-the-East, a sudden surprise when you reach the top of the steps. Hawksmoor's empty shell stands there, visible from afar like all the others. The middle was destroyed by a bomb and a small modern church stands within the shell.

On then to us. If he does not come by himself, he is brought by his architecture boss.

'Please lock the door when you are all inside,' I said one day to a lecturer with a group.

'Oh, that'll be all right,' she told me airily. 'We shall only be in there for about ten minutes.'

Ten minutes? For all those budding architects to appreciate line and curve, height and balance, splendour and decay?

'It only takes about ten seconds to walk out with a calor gas stove or a pair of candlesticks,' I replied.

If we can hand over the key without crossing our front

door step, well and good. Being curators of an ancient building is a time-consuming job. But there are many days when we have to go over there ourselves with plumbers, organists—or the man to read the meters.

'Wet old day for you,' I said sympathetically to the meter man one morning.

'Ah, but interesting,' he said. 'I've just been reading the meters in the Tower of London.'

There was an American who had been curate here for a short while. I felt I ought to go over with him and show him round personally. As we came down the steps he pulled out a £10 note.

'That's not for the church,' he said sternly. 'It's for your husband to buy books for himself.'

And there was the only organist I have ever worried about. Usually they go into raptures when they see our organ and almost take to the air when they begin to play. This one remained impassive and merely said it wasn't bad. Something fishy about him . . . I reported him to our Diocesan organ chief.

So come with me down our garden path and turn left past the builder's merchants. Left again into St Anne's Passage but stand still for a moment. This is *the* view of the church, seen from the west.

It was built in 1730 for the growing population of London by a pupil of Christopher Wren. Parliament raised the money for this and forty-nine other churches, most of which were never built, by putting a tax on coal. I can hear half the congregation saying, 'Hypothermia to build it and hypothermia to sit in it!' Well, how do you heat adequately a space as large as this? Most things that Nicholas Hawksmoor built were huge. Heating bills and maintenance were matters that posterity, but not he, would worry about.

So, before you is a wide fan-shaped flight of steps, double oak doors, half a dome and above them all the massive tower. It rises impressively into the sky and you can see it from Whitechapel, Greenwich and Bermondsey. In the old days it was a navigation mark for sailors coming up the Thames; today it needs propping up and restoring.

Christopher wrote a hymn for our 250th Anniversary which begins,

> Towering over road and river
> Stands this house of prayer. . . .

and that describes it exactly. We go on along the narrow cobbled street and into the churchyard, but not up the great west steps. They are only for weddings and funerals because the oak doorway lets in enormous draughts, even on a summer's day. We go round, instead, to the north, where we had the door painted red as soon as we arrived, to show that the church was still open.

Once inside, it is the vastness that first impresses people. They find it difficult to admire or exclaim because they don't quite know how to put it. Is it magnificent or is it just huge and alarming? Architects say it is magnificent; the rest ask about heating bills. Or they look up at the plaster flaking off the cherubs and garlands high above and say, 'Oh dear, poor ceiling, when are you going to restore it?'

In 1923 gas lighting came to St Anne's. We have two handsome photographs of the interior 'taken by the aid of the incandescent lighting alone.' The globes were low, where they were needed. When electricity took over, visibility took a step backwards. The lights are high in the ceiling, not the best place for illuminating the small print in 'Psalm Praise'.

Replacing a bulb in any of the three clusters of lights is a lengthy two-man operation. One person goes up the tower into the roof-space, unplugs the connection and then turns a handle (when he has found it) to winch the whole thing down into the aisle where his accomplice is waiting to whip out the bulb, run a duster round the bowl and then put the new bulb in. Number one then winches it up again, plugs in and dusts himself down, hoping Mum won't notice that he lay on the floor in his best trousers. Yes, it's a job that our sons usually do and they've got it down to a fine art.

One spring-cleaning day when the church door was open, an American wandered in as they so often do, to look around. He was a little startled to find a chandelier at shoulder level and a young man yelling 'Lower, you idiot' towards the ceiling. Eeerily, the unseen celestial technician (who was Idle number two) bawled back, 'Keep yer 'air on, it's coming!'

The American took some photographs and then, stepping backwards to get a better shot, he tripped over the cluster of lights and tore his trousers. Later he met Christopher and told him what had happened next.

'I went into the pub for a drink and the guy said did I know I ripped my pants. So I said to him, "Yeah, I just did that. I tripped over a chandelier." And he kinda gave me a funny look. . . .'

Back in 1850 there was a fire on Good Friday caused by blocked flues in the boiler, and it gutted the church. The Victorian architect Philip Hardwick restored the building much as it had been before, which was very restrained of him. The eighteenth century went in for classic buildings, simple lines and clear glass windows. Then along came the Victorians with their curly lines, stained glass and sentimental carving. Our font is a prime example of this—drooping lilies all the way round it.

Thanks to Hardwick's restraint and his respect for the original, we have plain glass in all the windows except the east and a gallery round three sides of the church. If you knew All Souls', Langham Place, before it was altered you will have an idea of what ours is like—dark wood pews and dark wood pillars—only ours is taller!

Whatever the huge building stands for on weekdays—Hawksmoor's masterpiece or merely a conglomeration of masonry—'By the way,' said Robert Bowman our local builder, 'some of these stones are only staying up here by force of habit'—on Sundays it is the house of God for the people of God. I love Sundays, one of the busiest days of a busy week, when once more I meet my brothers and sisters in Christ.

Every first Sunday of the month, I play the organ. 'You've got to remember she's a very frail old grandmother, and treat her accordingly,' said our organ chief. But sometimes in the middle of a hymn, I want to kick her.

She is another masterpiece, built for the Great Exhibition of 1851. She won the Gold Medal and Queen Victoria heard her played. But what were Mr Gray and Mr Davison to do with their prize organ when the Exhibition was over? Limehouse Parish Church needed a new one after the fire; and so to Limehouse she came and up into the west gallery, bought for £800. A snip, even in those days.

Since then, an electric motor has replaced the hand blower, but otherwise nothing has been altered in these one hundred and fifty years. 'How wonderful!' say the organ enthusiasts. But I mutter other things when the weather has made it moody; the registration I used on a clear dry day, making the hymns crisp and bright, is no good on a wet day. So I have mixed feelings as I climb the stairs and switch on the motor.

While it warms up I kneel to pray and look over the edge of the gallery at the Christian family gathering below. A bit like heaven really—'Here from all nations, all tongues and all peoples. . . .' There's Belfast and Hong Kong, America and Australia, Nigeria and Ghana, and the West Indies, not forgetting Guatemala.

A vicar in the Kentish Bible belt asked me once if people in our church found it difficult to mix with newcomers; his own people did. We are such a mixture anyway that we are spared that problem.

Lovely to see the church building filling with the church family. The twins are arguing with their mother about which pew to have: Amy is bossing her father. Henry is handing around sweets and Pam is selling the Church of England Newspaper.

I always think of that pew on the right as Fred's. He liked an orderly routine and always sat in the same one. He was nearly seventy when he first ventured into church, just to see what it was like. He ventured again the next week, his orderly routine now disrupted by a hesitant quest for God. And he found the Person he was looking for.

He filled in a form so that his name could be put on the Church Electoral Roll, a mark of membership. The form stipulates that you must either live in the parish or have been attending the church for six months. Ignoring the fact that he lived in the parish, Fred said, 'I've only been coming for twenty four weeks, but there's another two before the form has to be in, so I hope that's in order.' He was confirmed after that and became a faithful member of the church of Jesus Christ.

One January evening his daughter rang.

'Dad's been in the bathroom a long time,' she said. 'The door isn't locked but I dare not go in. Could you come?'

We bundled into warm clothes and started slowly up the road over the frozen snow. Across the small embankment of black slush at the lights and on up Salmon Lane, striding outside the shops where the pavement was clear, and stepping gingerly on to the snow again.

We found Fred on the floor.

'Hallo Chris,' he said, in a kind of sleepy surprise. 'I couldn't get up again.' We lifted his head a little and then I rang for an ambulance. Christopher was talking to him when I got back.

'There's nothing to be afraid of,' he was saying. 'The Lord is with you, Fred. He's prepared a place for you in heaven.'

And so we knelt there with our arms round him while

his life ebbed away. It was hard to give him back to God when God had so recently given him to us.

Gradually the church on earth becomes the church in heaven; the dividing line between them gets narrower.

Here comes Derek, choosing a back pew as usual. He wandered into church one Sunday evening looking for help, for someone to say a prayer for his son. We had 'open prayer' after the second hymn that evening and Christopher came down among the pews to ask us who needed special prayer. 'Could you please pray for my son? He's in hospital with stab wounds. That's why I came in here,' said Derek. His son got better and Derek continued coming; he would slip into the back pew and then be first out at the end. Gradually his searching gave way to finding; he began to know Jesus Christ for himself.

It was during this phase that our evening services were interrupted a few times. A group of teenagers, looking for a laugh, used to come in and lark around. We tried all manner of gentle approaches, sitting with them, chatting to them before the service started but to no avail. Derek was always ready with a friendly word, but sometimes he had to be one of the chuckers-out. Christopher told them they couldn't come interrupting our services any more than they would let us come interrupting one of their parties, but if they liked, they could come on Tuesday.

So for a few weeks they came to a club on Tuesdays, but they don't stick at anything very long and so they drifted off again. What will happen to them? Will they be able to cope with life when they leave school? Will they meet anyone else who will show them the love of Christ?

Not everyone comes right into the building; one year the gang walked into the porch and stripped the Christmas tree, during the Carol Service. That was the first and last time anyone thought it was a good idea to have it in the porch.

And one spring morning, when Natasha was being baptised, Bobby James came into the porch. Natasha was one of my Explorers. She had decided at the age of ten to ask for baptism. We were all very happy about it. Christopher prepared Natasha, her mother prepared a family party. It was the sort of morning everyone looks forward to.

When there is a baptism I leave the organ and lean over the gallery a little to join in the responses; today I wanted to stand beside Natasha. As the family walked down the aisle to the font I fled across the gallery and down the stone stairs.

'Dear God, what shall I do?' I thought as Bobby stopped sniffing and took his face out of the bag of glue. He looked at me sheepishly and got to his feet and I knew it was a good sign and ran on. All in seconds. I arrived at the font to have Christopher murmur 'Water' to me. We had all been so busy that morning that we had forgotten it.

I went across to the coffee urn, dignified and quick, and brought back a jugful. But my mind was still churning—the joy and the ugliness, Natasha's shining eyes and Bobby's bag of glue; the bright bubble of the morning wearing a ball and chain.

We got to know Bobby a little after that; he wasn't into glue very far. Simply drifting because his sister had turned him out. Now he has moved away, one more memory of someone we made friends with for a few short weeks.

I slide on to the organ seat and pull down the angle-poise lamp to shine on the music. What shall we have for a voluntary on this spring morning? Behind me the sun is pouring in through the east window, making pools of red and blue light on the chancel floor.

I turn to the Easter section in the Anglican Hymn Book and launch into 'Ye choirs of new Jerusalem' for a warm-up. I listen, to try and gauge how the organ is feeling this morning. Wing comes to wind the clock which hangs on the gallery. Marcus suddenly appears and murmurs, 'Dad says, Can we have a verse of "Jesus loves me" after the baby's Thanksgiving?'

'Sure,' I murmur back. At our last Confirmation, Christopher changed a hymn in the middle of the service to fit in with the bishop's sermon. Afterwards, Richard the Area Dean said, 'I bet he wouldn't have dared to change the hymn if anyone else had been playing!' and Bishop Jim said, 'Do you still love him after that?' But I believe in having appropriate hymns; they ought to be part of the way the service is flowing, fitting into the theme and lifting us up to God.

And a service, however carefully planned beforehand, is a warm and living process. So I'm all for changing a hymn if it's the right response to the preaching. Today it is plain sailing and I save 'This joyful Eastertide' for a voluntary at the end.

On the Sundays when our organist Lyn is up in the gallery, I wear my other hat—an Explorer leader. All the children who come to church belong either to the creche or to Climbers (age three to seven), my crowd who are juniors, or to Pathfinders (age eleven to fourteen).

We belong to a nation-wide network of groups, which means that the leaders have access to resource material and training days, while the children can participate in Fun Days and Knockouts with other groups.

On any Sunday there might be twenty or thirty children in church for the first twenty minutes. They are part of the family and so, disturbing as they might be when they grumble, cry or dance on the pews, we believe they should be there. But after the second hymn, all that changes. There is a sort of friendly traffic jam by the font as they all converge at the back and go off to their own venues.

The Explorers zoom up the south aisle and hurtle down the crypt stairs. Shem stands by the heavy velvet curtain and pulls it across after us all.

We settle down around the snooker table and address ourselves to prayer—short sentences of thanks for holidays or the Bible, short requests for each other or the absent ones. When Ian had just come as a new leader, one of the Explorers prayed, 'Thank you God for Ian coming. Please help him to settle down.'

And when Buky's Dad came back from a long trip to Nigeria, someone prayed, 'Thank you God for Buky's Dad coming back from Nigeria. Please help her to enjoy having him at home again.'

There is nothing like praying in order to learn how to pray. The younger ones catch the idea from the older ones, with a little help from the leaders.

Then we get down to half an hour of learning together.

'So why do you think Paul got someone to write his letters for him?' I asked one day.

'Well Miss, maybe he couldn't read or write.'

Which taught me that I hadn't done my job properly. If I had described Paul's early life and education more thoroughly, Michelle would not have made that mistake.

You can never take anything for granted when you are teaching children. But when they say 'Why? . . .' you know they have been listening. It was Clive who said one day, 'Well Miss, Jesus is our only one, isn't he?' If that had been Basil I would have bounced straight back at him—'What do you mean by "our only one" Basil?' But for Clive it was enough that he had come that far, that in his own quiet way he had formulated a faith for life.

I used to leader Explorers on my own, which was bad for them and for me; I was in a rut. Then Ruth came along; she is a Welsh nurse with a flair for drama in every Bible story. Discussion gave way to action and even the shyest would consent to a non-speaking part, standing beside the king's throne perhaps, or being part of the group walking round the walls of Jericho.

Soon after Ruth came Colin, an ordinand who wanted

to learn how. I had to think through not only how I did things that way but why I did them at all.

They both moved on and now we have Alison who brings her recorder and gets them to sing something, and Ian who prepares the lessons with his wife Wendy. Those lovely sheep on the chart are hers. So we are a team, keeping each other on our toes.

At about eleven-twenty-five, when we have done most of our work and are busy completing the work sheets, there are footsteps on the stairs. We are being summoned back into church for the final part of the service. So again, the whole family is together at the time when we take Holy Communion.

Some children like to come up and have Christopher say 'God bless you' and some don't. There are enough of each sort for everyone to feel natural about it.

I shall never forget the Sunday when I had Thomas, escaped from his family, with me. He was three. We knelt together at the rail and as soon as Christopher blessed him, he turned to me, small face alight with happiness, and silently put his hands on my head. I felt blessed indeed.

After church, I confess my first thought is potatoes. We like a real family Sunday lunch and we like it at one, so I dash home and put the potatoes in to roast. Lucky to live so close, of course.

Then, with my mind at rest, I go back to the crypt where everyone meets for coffee. I try to speak to any newcomers in case they have gone before Christopher gets there. The table needs clearing up after Explorers and there is next week's lesson to check out with the other leaders. And sometimes—an unexpected treat.

Last week I walked around with a tiny bundle of joy, Laura Jane, weighing a mere six pounds, showing her off to everyone while her mother had coffee in peace. All the younger ones went for her hands immediately. They were small enough to fit on a fifty pence piece. Exquisite.

Christopher often comes down last, waylaid in the

church by those who are not stopping for coffee and yet want to talk to him before they go. At last he locks the red door, turns off the lights and comes down for a well-earned coffee. Taking a service and preaching are thirsty work.

Sometimes I go up into the church again before I go home, to do some small job I'd forgotten. Everything is quiet. There is a faint whiff of snuffed-out candle and a blob of wax on the polished table.

I remember the first time I came into the building. It was empty. Christopher and I had come to have a look. There were a couple of pigeons flapping around. The faithful few had been battling along during the extended interregnum but they were no match for all the bird-life and vandals. So there were broken windows uncountable and dead pigeons nobody wanted to count.

We looked into the high tower rooms and the shadowy chancel, the silent vestries and the unused aisles. The building was full of little sounds and echoes, unfamiliar and daunting. I came out into the warm sunlight with icy hands; I was terrified.

Being a vicar's wife does not give one the ability to cope with everything. Being a Christian with a day-to-day working faith in God's love, Christ's salvation and the helping power of the Holy Spirit does not mean that one is never afraid. But it does mean that we can find God's grace to help in time of need.

During our first month here a party of students came to look around. After I had shown them the church, we ended up in the vestry looking at an old map.

'Thank you very much for showing us around,' said the leader. 'I think we'll be on our way now.' 'Oh, don't leave me!' I exclaimed. 'Sorry, that sounds daft but I'm not used to being in this building on my own yet. Can we walk to the door together?' So we did.

After a few months I was able to face going into the church alone, and nowadays I can pop in when it's dark, not even bothering to turn the power on and then the lights. I manage with a torch among the deep shadows and little echoes. It all took time. God does not magic our fears away.

This morning, the spring sunlight pours in through the south windows, falling on the dark pews and red carpet, glancing off the lectern and making a pool of light on the polished floor. There is a sense of peace. Almost tangible.

3

Fire!

They have set fire upon thy holy places and have defiled the dwelling-place of thy Name, even unto the ground.
O God, how long shall the adversary do this dishonour: how long shall the enemy blaspheme thy Name, for ever?
(Ps 74:8, 11)

'I was wondering during the service where my surplice was, and then I realised *you* were wearing it!' said David dryly. He was our Reader until he moved to his retirement house. They were in the vestry taking off their uniform—Christopher who puts on whatever is nearest, and David who had had to make do with the spare surplice.

So where was Christopher's? we asked ourselves. Slowly the answer dawned. He had been using the spare for several weeks without realising it, ever since the grandfather clock was stolen from the vestry. Wrathfully we put two and two together. The clock thieves had wrapped the grandfather in Christopher's surplice!

It is always the little things that sharpen the sense of loss. A valuable grandfather clock whipped over to the Continent, wrapped in a well-worn surplice. The music centre from our sitting-room and our tenor recorder, taken by thieves who trampled my precious rhubarb when they climbed over the wall.

I go cold with fear if we mislay the church keys; and

whenever the church is broken into I experience all the symptoms of physical shock—feeling sick, hands and feet icy cold. I cry, and come bedtime it is difficult to get to sleep.

'But it's not *your* worry,' says someone. True. The church building is the responsibility of the rector and the church wardens. And when the church wardens are on their way to work on the bus and the rector is away at a conference, it is the rector's wife who discovers the latest break-in. How do the burglars know when the rector is away? That is one of our unanswered but pertinent questions.

I phone the architect, any church warden who is at home, the police, and then with shaking hands make myself a cup of tea. Jesus said not to be anxious and not to have treasure here on earth where thieves break in and steal, but if you are the curator of an historic building you have to take care of it as best you can.

One Thursday when Christopher was away, I had this feeling that I ought to walk around the church. Thursday is our day off and time and again Wednesday night is when the vandals get busy.

I went into church and looked around. Nothing. I walked down the north steps, my knees already feeling weak with premonition, and turned left. I skirted the great west steps in the bright sunlight, looking up at the windows. And there on the south side—surely it was just the sunlight making patterns after the rain? No. The wire guard had been wrenched away. Pane after pane of glass had been broken. Once more the nightmare had become a reality.

As I unlocked the inside door of the west porch and showed the young policemen in, I caught sight of Iris's poster, put up on Sunday as a visual aid for her group. 'God is almighty, God is all loving' it said.

'So why did you let this happen, Lord?' I asked. The young bobby was complaining about his aching feet and

I was crying, wishing God would put the world right, not starting with me.

At least there was no further damage. The inner door of the west porch had been locked. It was merely the windows.

There was a time when we had no lock on the inner door and we nearly lost the church.

It was a warm May evening in 1978. Our church school had just put on a colourful production of 'Oliver' and we wandered homeward down Salmon Lane humming snatches of song. There was no preminition to dry our mouths; we were carefree and just slightly thirsty. Tim came in soon after the rest of us; he had been playing cricket at his school. The doorbell rang.

'That's Fiona. I'll get it,' said Christopher.

'I'll put the kettle on,' I said. Ring, ring. Bang, bang.

Christopher quickened his pace to the door. It was not Fiona. It was a young mother from the flats down the street. She had a baby in her arms and a toddler clinging to her skirt.

'Quick, oh quick, the church is on fire,' she said, breathless and frightened. 'I saw the flames from the window. It was awful.'

One of us rang the fire brigade, I can't remember who, and then I was on the church steps, waiting while Christopher went inside. He came out, smoke-blackened. 'I can't breathe in there and I can't see anything,' he said. And then the deafening, engulfing clamour of the fire engines racing round the block and into the churchyard. There was no more blessed sound in the world at that moment.

They were very quick. A few firemen in breathing apparatus were soon able to locate the three fires and put them out. That was merely the beginning of the night's work.

As we pieced together the evidence later, we realised what had happened. The arsonists, who must have been quite small, had pulled away the wire guard on one of the windows, broken a pane and climbed in. No easy task. Then they had lit a fire at the font, where all the hymnbooks are kept. This one only smouldered. They lit another in a chest of drawers up by the vestry where we kept papers and cardboard for visual aids. This was the blaze that our neighbour saw through the church window.

A third fire had engulfed the cupboard where the coffee things were kept for our drinks after church on Sunday mornings. We had a few dozen plastic cups for spares and it was the acrid black smoke from these that was now filling the church. Underneath the cupboard, the wooden floor was a charred ruin. So then came the lengthy task of clearing the smoke and checking the building.

I have no idea what I did for the next two hours. I know I wandered back to the house and found the boys looking after Fiona. I made her coffee but our usual warm hugs and eager talk seemed to belong to another world.

I must have gone back to the church after dark because it was then that I found John, Michael and Julian there. John lived in our street at that time. He believed in preserving ancient buildings and had bought his house because of the magnificent view of the church from his back windows. His friend Julian was also impressed with our building and he is now our architect. Hand in glove with the two of them was Michael who knows a lot about organs and antiques. They had all abandoned their evening cocoa and come to be with us, Julian was in a boiler suit, consulting with the firemen. It was greatly comforting.

John had also been in touch with Fleet Street so it was no surprise when *The Times* and *The Guardian* rang at about 11.30 pm to ask what was happening. I said we would ring back and ran across to the church, suddenly glad of something to do. The firemen were still extracting smoke; the neighbours and sightseers had dispersed.

'We're just coming over,' said Christopher. So back in our kitchen I made coffee for him and the others and asked if there was anything else I could do. 'Go to bed. And go to sleep. One of us needs to be awake in the morning. I shall be in church for hours yet, seeing to things.'

So I went, committing the night to God and receiving his peace. While I was falling into bed, something good was happening in church. Christopher and the others prepared to say a Psalm together, but first Michael decided that he would dare to try the organ and see if it was damaged. So at midnight, amid the smoke-blackened walls and damaged beams, the charred woodwork and the heartbreak, there pealed out:

> Praise to the Lord,
> the Almighty, the king of creation. . . .

strong and clear and in tune.

Next day, the ground floor of the rectory was covered with books from church—hymn books, prayer books and Bibles. They needed cleaning or drying. Those that were not scorched or sooty were wet from the hoses. The telephone rang constantly. Inevitably the local paper wanted a story. We drank coffee but didn't want to eat. It was like a bereavement.

In church a devoted squad of members worked through the morning, clearing the worst of the damage.

Tomorrow there was to be a wedding. Christopher went to call on the bride. Would she like him to buy a licence and marry them at St Dunstan's, next church down the road? No, she wanted to be married in St Anne's, come what may.

Just before lunch-time I went up to school with a church news-sheet, full of stop-press news, to be duplicated. Our duplicator had been destroyed in the fire.

On the way up Salmon Lane I stumbled, recovered, and looked down in surprise. Was this me walking up the street in broad daylight? Old shoes and paint-splattered trousers, a grey top that had been pink when I put it on, and grey arms. No doubt my hair and face matched, but I didn't even bother to look in a shop window and find out.

Peggy, the school secretary, sweet and courteous as ever, made no comment.

'I'll ring you when they're ready,' she said.

I think we slept during the afternoon and woke when the boys came in from school. There was more work to do in the church after tea, if it was to be anything like ready for the wedding and the Sunday services. When I went over, there was a man standing with his back to me. I knew that back and the stoop of those shoulders. Once, years back, I had been crossing a main road near here—kerb to bollard to kerb—and the same again across the road at right angles, behind an old tramp. When we both reached fourth base, I realised he was the vicar of the church beside whose door we had arrived.

More recently, I was pouring coffee at some Deanery meeting in our Crypt Room and he came to the hatch in urgent need of a safety pin. I did a quick rummage and sent him away happy with my last nappy pin, long hoarded, holding together the remnants of his tattered trousers.

We can laugh again after a while; thank God for old friends to laugh with. And here he was, pottering in to voice his concern, his rosy old face full of sympathy.

'I heard about the fire. Just wanted you to know how sorry we are, and we'll be thinking of you.' And he pottered away again.

The bride and her family arrived with brooms and buckets, eager to do battle with the grime. Neighbours dropped by with sympathy and offers of help. The golden evening brightened in the west. We slept well that night.

Next morning we went about our work dry-eyed and weary. John came up our path with an armful of irises from his small garden. You need friends to think of the obvious at times like that. I added every peony from our garden and made two glorious splashes of extra colour in front of the choir stalls.

When the bride was interviewed by the local paper, one of the things she said was, '. . . and the church was full of flowers. . . .' Not strictly true but a tribute to John's imagination on that leaden day.

Sunday was hard to get through. Everyone was saying, 'How did it happen?' and covering the ground that some of us had already covered in the last two days. The questions, the regrets, the shock and sorrow, the anger and the misery. I stood there crying after church, wishing we could have a press conference and get it all over.

I cried rather a lot for the next fortnight. How could we go on? I wanted to run away. Maybe God was calling us to another parish.

Tears, however, are not just a part of the mourning; they are part of the healing. Gradually I found that I could, after all, go on.

None of us wore our best clothes to church that summer. Every time we sang a hymn, tendrils of soot came floating down from the ceiling. They landed on our open hymnbooks, on our hair, on the pews. There was nothing we could do but be patient.

A few weeks later, one Saturday evening, Christopher and I were saying Evening Prayer together. The Psalm for the day was Psalm 74, which talks about enemies vandalising the house of God and setting it on fire. After a couple of verses I began to cry.

Christopher came out from his reading-desk and put his arm round me—though there is no provision for this in the Prayer Book.

'Come on,' he said. 'We'll say it together.' So we

stumbled through, feeling again the pain and the desolation and receiving a fresh measure of healing.

Nine years later, you can still smell the charred wood up by the vestry. And until we changed our Service Book, I felt a pang every time I laid the table for Holy Communion and found the place—the page for the Thanksgiving was begrimed where it was lying open on the night of the fire.

Yet here we are, still standing, by God's grace a worshipping community in Limehouse.

4

Crypt in the city

For one day in thy courts is better than a thousand.
I had rather be a door-keeper in the house of my God than to dwell in the tents of ungodliness (Ps 84:10, 11).

If there is one man who is guaranteed to fill me with alarm it is the manager of En-Con. That stands for Energy Conservation and his firm has done a lot of work on the heating in the church. Anyone who can improve the heating in a vast building like ours deserves a medal, but when the manager phones up and says their man is coming to look at the boiler tomorrow, my inside turns over. Christopher will be out tomorrow and so my treat for the week is to take the man down to see the boiler, in the crypt.

Since 1984 the journey has been much shorter than it used to be, a mere fraction of the space underneath the church. Beginning in daylight, we pass through the everyday, lived-in atmosphere of the Crypt Room and go through the pink door into the hidden world beyond.

The floor is uneven and there's a hole to watch out for as we turn the first corner. We go past walled-up chambers that contain lead coffins put there in the eighteenth century (these don't worry me a bit) and dark holes that are side passages. They seem to gape and sigh though they only contain piles of forgotten bricks or an abandoned shovel. Every hair of mine is standing on end, while the boiler man makes friendly conversation as if he found his way to boilers in surroundings like these every day. Turn left and there is the boiler room, with a proper electric light.

I leave the man there, happy to meet our boiler again. He says he can find his own way out and he'll be fine, thank you.

Trembling in the torchlight, I head for the pink door. I walk on the soft white dust of two and a half centuries and suddenly I am out again, between the table tennis table and the meal trolley.

Before our Crypt Room was made, the journey was a lot longer—more than half the length of the church, beginning in the dungeon under the vestry. It was all passages, dust, old forgotten tools and rubbish. The room under the choir vestry was piled from floor to ceiling with Scout equipment, decades old. We even found an invitation to a Garden Party at Buckingham Palace, addressed to a former curate. I wonder if he went? A trip to the crypt was one of the excitements of Limehouse for some of our family visitors.

'Oh how interesting, fascinating . . . can we really?' But it was Christopher who conducted the tours; I preferred to stay at home and put the kettle on.

During the war, the crypt was used as an air-raid shelter. Then for the next forty years it lay mainly undisturbed. But not totally. The Oxford students disturbed the dust once a year, and in 1980 Paul and Ruth took a table tennis table down there. It was not only difficult to get the great heavy thing along the narrow passages, but almost impossible to find an open space big enough to house it in all that vast cavern. Paul and friends put yellow paint on the walls surrounding this precious space, took a few chairs down and look—a den for the teenagers. It had to do for then; it was better than nothing at all. But what riches we have now in comparison.

The Oxford students, different each time, came once

a year for several years—a small working party who did painting and maintenance work on the church, lived in homes around the parish and learnt, just for a week, what Limehouse looks like. They did valuable and dirty work up in the tower, clearing out sacks of numerous dead pigeons and putting chicken wire across the spaces where they came flapping in.

In those early years we had hideous corrugated iron across all the crypt windows; one year the students painted it all olive green, rendering it almost invisible.

One night after a group of students had departed, Christopher and I lay in bed talking about the past week. 'You know what?' I said. 'Now there are women in the college, they'll be writing next year to say "Can we bring some girls?" '

'What shall we say?' asked Chriostpher.

'Have to say No,' I said. 'I don't know anything about girls. Suppose one of them was homesick or something? I wouldn't know what to do.'

But they did not write the following year and ask if they could bring any girls. They sent a list of the names of those who were coming, reading alphabetically—Carl, Chris, Colin, Laurence, Maureen, Phil. Now we look back, it was one of the best groups we ever had. That was the olive green paint year.

Colin came back to us for two years before going to college again and then being ordained. Paul and Ruth have been with us for years; he was in the first-ever Oxford week. Others have come back at different times or kept in touch, all adding to the flavour of Limehouse.

The students also invaded the crypt on errands. One year it was a search for long-forgotten candlesticks for the Carol Service. Another year they knocked one of the breeze-block walls down to ease the journey of the table-tennis players. Dust and grit wafted up the stairs and lay heavily all over the vestry after this effort. And every year there were bits and pieces of wood and old furniture which had been cluttering the church, to take down and store in the limitless space below.

All that space under there and space was what we needed. We had no church hall and were often thankful. No church hall to be vandalised or worried over, we often said.

Just opposite the church is a huge ugly Victorian building—'So ugly that it's beautiful' someone once said. Everything used to happen there—Scouts, Brownies, Mothers' Union, fetes and jumble sales. Gradually it fell into disrepair, the church membership dwindled. Rats invaded and floorboards subsided. To everyone's great relief it was sold just before we arrived. Now it just stands there, waiting for someone to have a bright idea about it. 'Limehouse Church Institute' is carved over the front entrance, but fortunately it is ours no longer.

So when we came, everything happened in the church building or in our house. Coffee after the morning service was always a traffic jam. The Explorers group had to run across to the rectory, rain or shine, every Sunday. The Church Council and every other committee met in the rectory—dining room, sitting-room or study according to the size of meeting. Often it was the sitting-room, which was hard on our boys when there could be three or four meetings in some weeks. They did their homework in their bedrooms but there wasn't much chance for them to put a record on and relax.

Parish parties and get-togethers had to be planned very carefully and were squashed-up affairs in the rectory or the west porch. Parish lunches were a great feat of organisation—we ate them in the gallery.

'Wouldn't you like a church hall?' people often asked. We were not sure. Given the total vandalism in Limehouse, it would have been a daunting prospect.

When the change came, it seemed to happen overnight. In reality, work had been going on for many months. Julian our architect had been surveying the crypt, drawing plans, prodding brickwork. He and our Care for St Anne's committee had put together a statement about making a meeting room in the crypt. The London Docklands Development Corporation were making grants to improve the amenities of Dockland and benefit the community. Did we qualify? Years of painstaking work were coming to fruition. Yes, we were to have a grant!

One morning Dove Brothers, Builders, put up their sign in the corner of the churchyard and a lorryload of scaffolding rumbled across the tarmac at the back of the church.

The east wall was to be repaired and cleaned, while the first three bays of the crypt were to be made into a parish meeting room. Work had begun!

The inner walls were knocked down and the coffins removed, to be reburied in a local cemetery. Carpenters and plumbers whistled and sang where the spiders had lived undisturbed for so long. Instead of pale green paint on wartime brick, the old eighteenth century brick piers emerged, warm and red in the glare of a string of electric lights.

Christopher was always coming back delighted with his latest look at progress. My own glimpses were usually on my way shopping when I would call in with a letter for Dove Brothers or a parcel —

'Would you mind?' our regular postman would say. 'I've pushed the door and looked around but I can't make anyone hear.' Sometimes it would be an odd pay packet, once it was a vital small part the plumbers were waiting for.

There came an afternoon when I went over there with a message, to find Alf the foreman hugely pleased. He offered to show me around.

'We've dug it all out now,' he said, going ahead of me between raised flagstones and piles of builders' gear. At first sight of Alf's bulk and greying hair, you might think he was a bit tottery, but see him moving surefooted around the cluttered site and you knew he was in charge. I followed him under an archway and he pointed to the dry channels dug in the floor.

'Now this here is the—er—Ladies, and over here, this is going to be the Gents.' A year later, when some of us went on a visit to Lindfield, where the church prays for us, I asked Winnie to say a bit about our new Crypt Room.

'Well!' she said. 'How we ever waited two hundred and fifty years for a toilet I don't know.'

The Crypt Room was only a part of the project in which the grant from the London Docklands Development Corporation was being used. Their brief was, and is, to improve the environment of Docklands. So the outside of the church was also changed, with a face-lift in two stages. The stonework was sandblasted, iron cramps put in by the Victorians were taken out again, having rusted, and the broken stones restored.

When the scaffolding finally came down, there was the creamy Portland stone in all its former splendour, with the grime of two hundred and fifty years removed. Twice in the next week I collided with someone in Three Colt Street; we had each been walking along looking up at the church.

'Lovely, isn't it? Fancy all that carving being up there and we never knew . . .' Anyone walking along there was liable to be on a collision course, enjoying the clean new look of the east wall. The whole neighbourhood was delighted.

By Palm Sunday the kitchen was taking shape. You won't believe this but during the planning stage, someone from the London Dockland Development Corporation asked why a church meeting room needed a kitchen.

Then suddenly, after Easter, the number of workmen seemed to dwindle. After all the excitement of the excavations and the main building work, the smaller items seemed to be taking much longer to finish. Would we be able to have the opening in May as we had planned?

A week before Opening Day the builders still had a lot to do.

'And that's the understatement of the century,' said Christopher. They suddenly speeded up and finally on that Tuesday they stuffed all their gear into the unused end of the crypt, through the pink door.

As we put out chairs we found a broken one. 'Let's put it in the junk-hole,' said someone, opening the door. The builders' clobber reached right to the opening, with a wheelbarrow as the last thing they had pushed in and there was no room, even for a chair.

All the questions that had exercised us for weeks past were suddenly left in abeyance as we prepared the room. 'What shall we call it? What shall we do about new chairs? Can we say in writing what we shall use it for?' They would have to be thrashed out later; tonight the show must roll.

Having set out a fan-shaped auditorium of odd chairs, we went home to take off our old clothes, wash our dusty faces and put on our best clothes for the ball. Vicars' wives, more than most, have to turn up looking as if all they ever did is to sit on a cushion and sew a fine seam and feed upon strawberries sugar and cream, but like everyone else, they were actually washing the dishes five minutes ago. A church member once found me on hands and knees in the vestry, soon after the fire.

'Oh, Mrs Idle, it doesn't seem right,' she said, 'seeing you here scrubbing the floor. "The rich man in his castle, the poor man at his gate"—that's how I was brought up.' Well sister, things are different now. I laughed and said we were all in the same boat here, everyone could do a bit to help.

In the crypt, on that May evening, the first arrivals were looking around at the warm brick walls, the exhibition of 'Before and After' photographs and the smart fitted cupboards in the kitchen. The architect's assistants were drilling holes in our lovely walls to put up a mounting for the photographs.

I accosted visitors as they came down the steps.

'It's nice to see you. Where are you from?' I said.

They were consultant engineers, assistant surveyors, the man in charge of the open spaces in the borough. I had no idea how many experts are involved in a new building. And here was Alf the foreman in a smart grey suit and looking hugely pleased, as always.

There were not quite enough chairs in the end for all those who came. Last of all, to their reserved seats came the Care for St Anne's committee who had been holding a short meeting to settle details before they met the public. Christopher welcomed us all, the Archdeacon said a prayer and the Crypt Room was open.

Julian has a way of talking about the finer points of the building that makes it all vividly interesting. We were immersed in crumbling stonework and rusting iron cramps when two shadows crept down the stairs and slid into the kitchen. One was buxom and had its hair in a bun; the other was square like a meat-tin. Mary West, with a tray of chicken legs cooked in her inimitable flavoursome West Indian style.

Julian gave place to Michael whose genial manner and witty asides kept us as engrossed as Julian's technicalities. But gradually a spicy aroma began to drift across our nostrils. Gastric juices began to flow. Wasn't it time that Michael stopped? He did and we were soon enjoying a typical Limehouse spread. Why do we want a kitchen indeed!

Come outside for a minute and look through the window. They are all in there, being polite to people they have never met before and keeping an eye open for another cup of coffee. Over their heads, the electric lights are set into the sides of the pillars, pointing upwards. The vaulted brick ceiling, mellow and rosy, catches the full beam and reflects it downwards, warm and soft on to the heads below.

Unlike the vast white edifice above, rising into the evening sky, the Crypt Room looks cosy and inviting. Come on, let's go back and help with the coffee cups.

It was named the Crypt Room but we tend to be lazy and call it the crypt. All the things that happen in most church halls happen down there—Bible study groups and Explorers, coffee after church and meetings of every kind. The Ragged School Museum Trust held an exhibition down there and when the Limehouse Development Group held a Limehouse Festival in the churchyard, Em Sharp and her helpers served endless cups of tea to the neighbourhood from our crypt kitchen.

We have learnt how to manage the power points now; you can have three on in the kitchen but if you stick something into the fourth, the fuses blow. Christopher met a member of the East London Baptist Tabernacle the other day.

'I came to your church once,' she said. 'And when we went downstairs for a cup of tea all the lights went out.' I hope she will come again now that we have learnt to do things better.

At the entrance to the crypt is a plaque, commemorating the opening of the Crypt Room. On the silky smooth Welsh slate are engraved the names of the architect and the builder, Wendy Byworth our former parish worker who left a bequest, and the two churchwardens, Iris Bryzak and Rose Ali.

Women have always found plenty to do in our church, using their gifts to the full. We have almost always had one woman churchwarden but rarely two.

Iris grew up as a Baptist in Bow and I remember meeting her for the first time—in a plum-coloured winter cloak.

She was a Social Worker and joined our church in Poplar; and so did this Aussie whose parents had fled from post-war Europe to Brisbane. He had come over for a few weeks' holiday and work experience.

And here they still are—a multi-ethnic family you

could call them, but you might get a funny look if you did. Our church family is incomplete if Nick, Iris, Alex, Michael and Adrian are not around.

Rose married young and brought up seven children. If you went to visit her you would find the flat full of grandchildren, with a dog or two for good measure. Neighbours as well. The little flat in Christian Street overflowing with humanity was a place where people in the block could come for crisp advice, a cup of tea and maybe a good cry. The block was a better place for having that Christian oasis there.

'Do you know what Rose and May and Marguerite all have in common?' asked Christopher one day.

'Not sure. Do they all live in the same block? Did their children all go to the same school?' I didn't say they would all take up a good deal of room on the back seat of a taxi.

But the answer was—all their surnames are Ali. These three real East Londoners had stuck together as friends, caring for each other in hard times and helping their good-looking children grow up in a sometimes hostile world.

When Rose put in for a smaller and newer flat, she met delay and disappointment because her name was Ali. Unlike many another Ali, however, Rose was able to turn to her Rector who wrote a letter to the Housing Department. Soon after, she was able to move into a lovely little flat nearer the church.

She was active in the Tower Hamlets Association for Racial Equality, able to see the issues from two viewpoints—that of an East Londoner born and bred, and that of a partner in a mixed marriage who had experienced the frustrations of the immigrant population.

What with the Racial Equality Association and being a churchwarden, Rose got to know our bishop, Jim Thompson, quite well. At a big service in St Paul's

Cathedral one day, she whispered to her granddaughter,

'Look, there's my friend Bishop Jim.' Her granddaughter was cynical.

'Garn, Gran. 'E ain't your friend. How can 'e be your friend?'

Next time Rose met the bishop, she told him. And Bishop Jim sent her a small card to show to her granddaughter. It said, 'To my friend Rose, from Bishop Jim.'

I remember another thing that happened to Rose. (Things always did.) It was at a Family Service. We had been having a 'Family Feature' and at that particular service it was Gillian Ali the youngest and Rose, standing up there at the front.

'What about your job, Rose?' asked Wendy the interviewer.

'Well, I like working at the London Hospital, it's a very nice place,' said Rose. 'But the job I'm doing at the moment is really horrible. It's early morning cleaning on a ward that I don't like. But I'm going to stick at it and watch out for a transfer.'

At the back of the church sat Rose's supervisor who had come that morning to hear her daughter's banns read. It was the only time she had ever been in our church. Next morning she sent for Rose.

'I was in your church yesterday morning and I heard what you said. . . .' Rose broke into a sweat. ' . . . and I'm arranging for you to have a transfer on to the Intensive Care Unit.'

Rose loved it there; she watched over the patients as if she was the ward sister herself. She would ask us to pray for them at the prayer meeting. Or more often, for the relatives in their distress.

It was while we were on holiday in Belfast in 1985 that someone rang to tell us Rose had died suddenly. Christopher flew home to take the funeral.

Rose in heaven is so much a part of our life here as a

church family; we find it difficult to believe that she won't be here next Sunday.

I'm glad her name is on the plaque.

5

Up and down the City Road

God is our hope and strength: a very present help in trouble.
Therefore will we not fear, though the earth be moved and
though the hills be carried into the midst of the sea.
Though the waters thereof rage and swell . . . (Ps 46:1–3)

Christopher's voice said, 'Are you asleep?' I had heard that tone of voice before and it meant Help! It was about eleven o'clock and I had gone to bed, leaving him working in the study. I clambered up out of the dark comfortable hole that had been my first sleep and said, 'Wassup?'

'There's a young man on the front door step who's cut his hand quite badly. I've phoned for an ambulance.' I came downstairs, stomach churning, praying for strength not to faint.

'Couldn't you send them somewhere else sometimes, Lord?' I asked unreasonably. 'Why is it always the rectory? And you know I'm not very good at the sight of blood, in spite of being a nurse.'

Outside the front door, in the warm evening, Brian was sitting on a kitchen chair, holding out one hand. Blood was pooling on the step. I pressed both my thumbs into his wrist and slowly the trickle subsided. I asked him what had happened but neither of his two stories rang quite true.

He had not long been out in the world—out from the

children's home where he had grown up, and he had little idea of how to cope with life. He began sobbing and hid his face on my shoulder.

'What's going to happen to me?' he said.

'Oh, they're ever so nice,' I said. 'They just stitch up the cut and put a comfy bandage on.' I went on chatting about the kindness of hospital staff, soothing him.

One thumb would do for the wrist now and I put an arm round him. Our cat wandered out to see what was going on; Brian talked to him and relaxed a little. He liked cats, he said. Christopher came out, a bowl of cornflakes in his hand. He had been pouring his regular vitamin-packed night-cap when Brian came to the door. It was high time he ate it, before it went soggy, but the ambulance driver might need a wave in our untidily-built street.

So while the ambulance flashed and wailed around our one-way system, there occurred one of those classic Limehouse moments. A young man on the steps being comforted by a woman in a dressing-gown and the rector of the parish church standing in the middle of the street eating his cornflakes.

We handed Brian over to the ambulance man and waved goodbye gratefully. An older friend would be at home in Brian's digs by the time he returned.

I carried the empty bowl indoors, washed the steps down and peace fell on the rectory.

The heat of July can bring a crop of accidents. With no fields or woods to play in, and Victoria Park a bus ride away, children grow bored and careless. They turn to daring pursuits like climbing on to the roofs of derelict buildings.

Near the end of one summer term, Jason and friends decided to play cops and robbers across the roof of an empty warehouse down our street. But the roof gave way and Jason fell through it to the floor far below. He had to be rescued by firemen. He was still alive; amazingly he only had bruises and broken bones.

He was one of my recorder players and I went to visit him in hospital. The bold roof-explorer looked very tiny lying in his white bed, but he was still full of chat.

For once, I thought about writing a poem, a kind of lament for all the children in Limehouse with nowhere to play. It began —

> Jason, Jason,
> Plummetting through warehouse roof
> By Limehouse Basin. . . .

but it never got any further. There was Barry to visit. Barry and his mother and sister went to live in the Women's Refuge for a while because father was coming home drunk so often and knocking them about. While they were there, Barry went to put the kettle on one evening and somehow caught his jersey alight.

He was so badly burned that they took him to the special Burns Unit in the Military Hospital on Woolwich Common. He wasn't a recorder player but I knew him. Somehow we had got friendly at school when he was in trouble one day. So I went to see him. The journey took an hour or so by bus, a quarter of an hour if someone gave me a lift. It was worth it to see his face light up when I walked in.

His father was shaken by the accident and the family was reunited after that. An uneasy truce; I am never sure of my welcome when I call there.

And then, that same summer term, as we sat over tea one day at home, I mentioned that Barry's sister had fallen over in the playground that afternoon. Quite by accident, someone had cannoned into her and sent her flying.

"But that could happen to anyone,' said Jonathan. 'Why the fuss?'

'Well, she didn't seem to have the oomph to recover normally,' I said. 'Poor little mite, there's nothing of her.

She's like a little fairy. She was so grey and dazed, she's staying in hospital overnight for a check up.'

'I don't understand it,' said Jonathan. 'All these kids in your school, having all these accidents.' As he spoke an ambulance began a deafening wail at the traffic lights fifty yards up the street, hemmed in by the rush-hour.

Are inner city children more accident prone than others? Do the pressures of life make them careless? Or was it simply a bad patch in the life of our school?

We heard the ambulance tearing round the block; it stopped wailing at the bottom of our street. Next day I found out that it had come for Lee, one of the second-year juniors. He had run into the road for his ball, straight into the path of a car.

'He's in that place Miss.'

'What place?' I asked my Sunday morning group.

'That place where you go when they don't know if you're going to live or die.'

'Do you mean the Intensive Care Unit?'

'No Miss. Acoma. He's in Acoma.' Oh, I see. We talked about comas and prayed for Lee. A few weeks later we were able to give thanks that he had recovered.

As a family, we have been very fortunate. Most of our visits to hospital have been to see friends. The London Hospital has brown industrial carpeting in the entrance corridors, doing away with that tremendous echoing clatter you often hear when visitors pour in. St Andrew's has the great grandfather of all long corridors.

'Progress,' said Miss Agnes Hill at the Methodist Church, 'or at least so-called progress, is four men cleaning that corridor with a machine. My little friend across the road—she's ninety now—used to be one of the cleaners up at St Andrew's. It was two women's work each day. They started scrubbing at each end and met in the middle outside Matron's office.' It is Christopher's daydream to throw a cricket ball down that corridor from one end to the other without it hitting the wall on its way.

Mile End Hospital has had a new entrance and an update since we came here but it is still the friendly neighbourhood hospital.

And St Clement's? St Clement's is the local psychiatric hospital, small and familiar. The only trouble is, none of the staff wear uniform and sometimes you honestly cannot be sure who is which. A tall man in pyjamas who accosts you and says he is the doctor is easy. 'Thank you but the staff nurse knows I'm here,' you say. But young women in jeans watching the television are more difficult to classify.

One of our church members, George, has been in St Clement's for five years now. Sometimes he plays Fast Asleep when we arrive but on good days he loves a visit. 'I was so depressed on Tuesday afternoon,' said Christopher, 'that I thought—who can I go and see? So I went to see George, for a bit of sanity.' George appreciated that; he gave a gurgle of laughter when I told him what Christopher had said.

He comes to the top of the stairs to watch us go and we wave until the corner hides him. Then out past the drain that always smells of shampoo and into the roar of traffic in Bow Road.

So all the local hospitals have become familiar to us over the years as we have walked in—and out again. We had never set foot in Moorfields Eye Hospital, however, until one July evening.

It began on the Saturday morning. Christopher was rubbing his face.

'I've got shadows across my right eye,' he said.

'Does it hurt?' I asked sharply.

'No. Just that I can't see properly. Anyway, I don't want to miss this meeting today. Thanks for the packed lunch.'

He came home at teatime with hardly any vision in the eye. His sermons were prepared, he was ready for Sunday and wanted to be in church. We talked and prayed together and agreed that with the help of the family, he could tackle Sunday morning.

That afternoon I rang Moorfields.

'He should come in at once,' said the Sister.

Again we talked and prayed. Conventional medicine is usually God's instrument of healing and not to be disregarded. It was the very end of July, the fifth Sunday in the month. The evening service was particularly concerned with prayer for health and healing. Christopher had set his heart on being there. So we delayed for a few more hours and went to church again, expecting to receive strength and help.

During the service, two of the church leaders placed their hands on Christopher's head, praying in their own words for his healing. It was a moment to remember; the whole church praying for their minister and committing him totally to God.

An hour later, Lyn was driving him to hospital. The nurse covered his good eye and said,

'Now, just read the letters on that board, please.'

'What board?' asked the patient.

Another hour later, I too was being driven up the City Road, carrying an overnight bag for Christopher, and a notebook. He had a detached retina.

There was a long but reasonable delay before he was admitted to a ward; long enough for me to scribble down all the jobs I needed to do for him next day. Phone calls, visits, letters, a long list of acknowledgements to those who had sent money for the church Gift Day . . . and one call to make now from the hospital about a wedding in another church that he would not be able to conduct on Saturday.

We prayed together and I left him still jotting, thinking ahead about his work. I went straight to bed and slept; not so the next two nights when I sat in the study burning the midnight oil, getting the desk work done. Besides letters to answer and file, there was next week's Christian Comment for the local paper to be sent off. I had to decipher it from a half-blind scribble before I began to type it.

It began '"The light of the body is the eye"—and those words of Jesus will mean more for anyone who has sat where I sit now. . . .'

The last paragraph wound up Christopher's relaxed, on-the-spot comments about Moorfields and his new daily intake of the New English Bible with the Talking Book. It said —

> And although I have used modern services regularly for over seven years, when I shut my tired eyes and grope for words to pray with, it is the Prayer Book phrases that come flooding back ready for use, to bring me into the presence of God. I wonder if others share my experience?

As I typed it out in the small hours, I wanted to put 'Yes, me too!' at the bottom.

Monday morning came. I was not in the least surprised to hear that Christopher would go to the operating theatre at midday. Hadn't we been praying for him? Later we learned that people waited for days to have their retinas re-attached, because of the busy hospital schedule. We also learned that the surgeon had said that morning, 'Sister, I can't operate on that old chap with the cough; he's simply got to stop smoking before I can tackle him. Send the new patient—Mr Idle—instead.'

I often wonder about that old man; is he still smoking and coughing in a sightless old age?

Meanwhile I tried to leave my anxieties with God and tackled the household chores and Christopher's workload. The rain poured down.

'You've got a slate off,' said a caller, pointing to the roof above the front door. I rang the builders.

Probably the church ought to have a visit; the huge building was far from weather-proof in 1978 and buckets might be needed. Inside the north porch all was in order but I caught a sound. . . .

'O Lord, please help me. What shall I do? I can't go away and ignore it. My knees have turned to jelly. Please give me strength to walk through into the church. . . . I'm crossing the back of the church now. My tummy is screwed up so tight it hurts. Now Lord, whatever that waterfall sound is, I've got to push the door open and look at it. Prop me up Lord. . . . Yes, just as I thought, water cascading down the south-west stairs. Now I've got to go up the north stairs and see where it's coming from. Can I make it Lord? Couldn't I just go away? I'm so frightened. No, I'm the rector's wife and I must jolly well get on with it. Both the churchwardens are at work. I have to push this gallery door open now Lord. Strength to stand still in the face of panic, please. . . . Hmm . . . yes, I see, it's coming through the roof up there. Thank you Lord for helping me along. Now please could I get as far as the drain before I'm sick? . . . Here's the drain Lord, but I don't want to be sick now, I just want to cry.'

Back in the house, I rang Julian the church architect, to tell him about the waterfall. He thinks nothing of bringing dungarees and doing a bit of dirty work when necessary.

I cooked the dinner and thought of Christopher, lying under a green sheet with green-clad figures around him. He was in God's hands; so was I, the boys and the church family.

> The darkness is no darkness with thee, but the night is as clear as the day . . . when I wake up, I am present with thee (Ps 139:11, 18).

The afternoon brought the builders to do the slate, the architect to do the gutters and the Communion of Saints to assure me of God's care. Every Sunday we confess our faith—'I believe in God the Father Almighty . . . I believe in the Communion of Saints. . . . ' The saints on earth were very close to us, practical and loving, that week.

If anyone gave me a pious message of comfort, I don't remember it. What I do remember is—'When do you want me? I'll be there.' This was our old friend the Rev Vic Harper who was already poised to take over our house and parish when we went on holiday. He gladly took on an extra Sunday service.

I remember too—'Why don't you bring the boys round to our flat while you visit Chris?' and 'Why don't you all come to tea after visiting?' I am glad I took up both of those offers promptly because, to everyone's surprise, there were only two days in which to visit; such is modern eye surgery.

After that, the invalid came home with permission to go on holiday. He was as weak as a kitten, stooping and uncomfortable in strong light. We wondered what Moorfields had done to him but as time went on and Christopher improved, we were very grateful to them for doing it so promptly and so successfully. The following week we were due to go on holiday. This year, unlike many, it had all been fixed months ago and it was three weeks long. Exactly what we needed. We were tremendously grateful to God and to our friends.

Back in January, a friend had dropped by and we asked her to stay for lunch. After lunch we thought of something. We said, 'Could we stay in your cottage in the summer while you are away?' She was quite willing, though six Idles would be a squash.

Then she wrote in February and said that on thinking it over, it would be too much of a squash, so we could stay in her parents' house instead. They could go to their own cottage in Wales. We did hope that she had mentioned it to them!

All we had to do now was get to Liverpool. Tim could cope with anything British Rail might do to us, Jonathan was, and always is court jester; Jeremy would make sure we left nothing behind and Marcus appointed himself as the necessary Guide Dog. Ahead was all that God had already planned for us in this lovely house, ours for three weeks. Christopher could sit and rest all day, taking short walks when twilight fell. The boys could swim in the nearby school swimming pool and there was a family who played cricket in the evenings in the field at the back. They invited our boys to join them.

How do you describe a vicar who goes quietly about his work with his eyes open? The vicar of Great Meols—where we went to church—stood at the church door greeting the congregation as they emerged and said something I have never heard a vicar say to a visitor before. 'Are you keeping well?' he asked. So Christopher had no option but to explain, and the vicar simply said, 'I'll put you on the parish prayer list for the next three weeks.' It was so quiet, so straightforward; it showed concern without embarrassing us.

So we were strengthened and blessed and by the time we went home, Christopher was beginning to feel himself again.

'You've got to say Dad got better,' said Marcus, when he had read the rough draft as far as this. Thanks, Marcus. Yes, over the next twelve months Christopher regained most of the vision in his eye.

We look back with great thankfulness for all the love that people showed us at that time and for all the prayers that were offered up for us by the church family.

6

High summer

O ye mountains and hills, bless ye the Lord:
  praise him and magnify him for ever.
O all ye green things upon the earth, bless ye the Lord:
  praise him and magnify him for ever (Benedicite).

It was high summer. I sat down by the telephone, hands cold, and prayed once more.

'I don't think the girls in the Admissions Office would understand my problem Lord. Could they please all be gone to the canteen for tea, so that that nice man answers the phone?' He did!

'Thank you for your letter about my admission to hospital on Sunday,' I said. 'I'm sorry that I won't be able to come in.' The voice at the other end was calm and courteous. Its owner is a churchman and knows Christopher but I never did find out who he was.

'Right, I've got that down. What reason do you give?' This was the difficult bit.

'Well . . . um . . . well, the bishop is coming to tea. That's the reason.' I could hear him smiling.

'That's perfectly all right, Mrs Idle. I'll put "Business reasons",' he said.

Incredible as it will seem to anyone who has been on a hospital waiting list, I was given another chance a week later. So that Sunday dawned, unlike any Sunday I have known. I rushed around after breakfast, made sure that dinner was in good hands and that we had reached a common mind about clean shirts and socks. Then, as the church bell began to ring, I dropped my overnight bag into the bicycle basket and pedalled up the road. I passed members of the congregation. We waved regretfully.

There is a handy little corner off the car park at Mile End Hospital where you can lock your bike against the railings. I pushed the combination lock well round and walked into the hospital.

I was admitted, introduced to the other two new girls and given dinner. Time passed slowly, even with the life of Bertrand Russell, the Bible, and a pile of letters to answer. The truth is, I was worrying; not about the operation, a very minor, routine affair. A loving church family can deal with operations—on their knees.

Christopher came, shared my cup of tea and rode the bicycle home. A medical student came and gave me a thorough examination. She seemed a little disappointed that I was basically so fit, my complaint so minor. Poor girl, she would have preferred a few elusive symptoms to grapple with.

I was alone again. What was worrying me was that I was sure God had some job for me to do while I was in here and I didn't want to miss it. The ward was quiet; Carol, a busy housewife, was enjoying a good read. Brenda who worked nights was having a sleep. The fourth bed was empty. So where was my job?

I don't mean anything spectacular like preaching the Gospel to the whole ward! We believe that when you go into hospital your first job is to be a good patient. But in some quiet way, I was needed this week, not last week. At four-thirty a nurse looked in and a small party of us headed for the chapel—Kathy, Dorothy and I. There was a warm welcome. The small chapel was packed. It was strange to be so fit and well, someone who ought to be dashing around helping the less able, and yet be reduced to the level of the weak and helpless merely by wearing a dressing-gown. Was that what happened to our Lord when he came to earth?

Strengthened by the service, the three of us came back. And there she was. The fourth bed in our ward was now occupied by a tiny woman from Bangladesh. She was crying. Her husband was trying to comfort her. I started writing another letter, watching with half an eye. The husband came over.

'Madam, will you look after my wife? She does not speak English.' He didn't speak very clear English himself and I was thankful for the practice I have every week in school, listening for the differently placed emphasis, the swallowed vowels, and piecing them together to make a sentence. I promised I would do all I could to help. Her name was Rukia and she was grieving for the two toddlers she had left at home. We talked for a little while; I think the husband was embarrassed by his wife's tears. The family were practising Muslims and their Mullah was a very good man. And what did my husband do? Ah yes, he was no doubt a very good man too.

I promised to pray for Rukia and went off to a beef supper. Tomorrow was starvation day so we lingered a little, making the most of a good meal.

Rukia was crying when I came back, her egg supper uneaten. I sat with my arm round her for a little while and we talked to each other, uncomprehended by our minds but understood by our feelings. After a bit she dried her eyes and tried out my name. 'Mardar' she said with a smile.

There are one or two undignified little chores one has to do on admission to hospital. The nurses had spent quite a time with Rukia already but now they were busy admitting emergency patients. So I coaxed Rukia and we got the chores done.

This was my scene, being nurse, mother and actress-explainer to this tiny woman just like the Mums at school. The best moment was when she said 'Yes' to Ovaltine and we sat drinking it together.

I lay awake until midnight, listening to the clatter and bustle of the busy ward. The familiar rumble and judder of Commercial Road would have been more soothing. Then I went across to Rukia. She was crying again. I squeezed her hand and stayed with her until she waved me back to bed. I slept all night and woke in the warm grey dawn, suddenly aware of someone beside me. Rukia was waiting for me, too frightened to venture down the corridor on her own. So we went along together, her tiny, precise form dwarfed by my lumbering five foot nothing.

Later, I coaxed her with a milk drink. Operation day was to be long and boring for me, strange and frightening for her. I was on 'Nil by mouth' while she had to drink six pints of water for a scan. It was a relief when an interpreter arrived and made things simpler for her.

A little while before dinner—but not hers or mine—I went and clasped Rukia's hand for the last time that day, before we settled down for a snooze in our elegant white operation gowns. She went down to Theatre and came back; Carol went down and came back. Brenda enjoyed her meals because she wasn't going down until tomorrow. I slept all afternoon, drugged.

I woke to hear the supper dishes clattering and could not believe my ears. Finally and wide awake, at seven thirty, I went down to Theatre. The staff had been busier than usual but were still courteous and cheerful. I held out my hand and felt a prick.

> If I take the wings of the morning:
>   and remain in the uttermost parts of the sea;
> Even there also shall thy hand lead me;
>   and thy right hand shall hold me (Ps 139:8, 9).

A nurse patted my face and said, 'Wake up, it's all over.' I was alive, I was awake. The daily hospital miracle of resurrection had taken place again. It was only five-to-eight and there was Christopher waiting to visit me.

Rukia had a bad night, sick and in pain but surrounded with gentleness. Carol's blood pressure was giving cause for alarm, I gathered, as I drifted comfortably in and out of sleep. They gave me a delicious drink of water somewhere in the small hours.

In the morning it was my turn to be out of bed first, to stand beside Rukia and squeeze her hand. She smiled and then I was at it again, coaxing her with a drink.

Carol was on the mend. I felt no effects from my small operation, though I was glad not to be cycling home. Christopher would be coming to escort me; David was taking a twenty minute coffee break to drive us home. Life was good.

There was something else. It was June the fifteenth, 1982. I fiddled with the radio knob on the wall beside the bed and found the seven o'clock news as it began.

'Hey, listen everybody!' I said. 'The News . . . it's just coming through. . . . The Falklands war is over.'

Breakfast tasted good. Then we all skipped back to bed, some more agile than others, for the doctor's round.

'Yer all right,' said my Yorkshire-born registrar. 'Noothing nasty. You can go home this morning.' It had never occurred to me that I might not, or that they might find anything 'nasty'. I was deeply thankful.

By the time morning drinks came round, Rukia was sitting in an armchair, and more comfortable. Silly of me to have worried about the kind of job God would give me. I took her hand and said, 'Goodbye Rukia, God bless you.' She thought for a minute and then said carefully. 'Mardar. OK,' and she smiled.

For the next few Wednesdays I was back in school as usual. End-of-term began to take over, leaving me with diminished classes. Trips to the Tower of London and Greenwich Park. The netball team went to Haringey for a tournament. The Leavers' Concert loomed large.

Heat lingered on brick and stone; I longed for a breath of fresh air.

Going away on holiday together as a family has always been great. Spread around the countryside are friends who have trusted us with their homes while they were away. From Sussex to Inverness, Hampshire to Cumbria, I have kept house in greener surroundings than usual, and we have been free to come and go as we pleased. First with pram and toddlers, then with boys who roamed independently. Now it is a bonus if they can spend a few days with us.

John and Isabel were very generous with their house and Chichester was a favourite haunt when they lived there. It was in Chichester Festival Theatre that Timothy and Jonathan saw their first Shakespeare production—Julius Caesar, with lots of blood; and thunder, lightning and rain to run home through afterwards.

Robert and Dierdre's home in Oxford is another favourite, with magpies dancing on the lawn and a dog who took Marcus for long walks.

'Do you remember,' said Jonathan the other day, 'when we got to York for our holiday, Jennie had made me a rabbit jelly?' That was his eighth birthday; on his ninth we were en route for Wales. By the time he got to sixteen, we knew that whole-family holidays were nearly at an end and accepted an invitation to stay in Scotland. That summer, British Rail were almost a hundred per cent on strike and there was not a hired car to be had. There were rumours that the railways were going to close down for ever. We prayed for wisdom and decided to wait.

At last the morning came. We queued up at King's Cross behind a luggage trolley that said 'Not to be removed from Euston' and passed the time by buying books and drinking coffee. It's not the clothes that make our cases so heavy; it's the number of books my menfolk take.

I have never seen such a happy queue; everyone was so relieved that a train was actually running. It was scheduled to go to Newcastle with a strong possibility that it would continue to Edinburgh. Our friends in Glasgow said there was a good inter-city bus if we could get to Edinburgh; what would happen if the train stopped south of the border? I had brought enough food for a siege. At last the barrier was opened, and then, almost before we had shared out the pages of the *Times*, the train was moving.

It was sad to see the dead stations—York, Darlington, Durham, empty and forlorn. At five o'clock, Newcastle ought to have been humming with school children, shoppers and the first trickle of commuters. Instead—nothing. Would we all have to get out here and make our way to Scotland as best we could?

The public address system on the train started crackling:

'Ladies and gentlemen, your attention please. This train will continue to Edinburgh, stopping at . . .' British Rail was getting us there.

At Edinburgh the ticket collectors had had nothing to do all day and were relishing a little activity.

'Anyone for Glasgow?' they shouted. 'There's a train leaving at six-thirty.'

We were on our way! Two days in Glasgow and then on into the Highlands.

Once arrived at our holiday house, it was a twenty mile drive into Fort William to church. Twenty miles of Western Scotland with Loch Eil beside us and Ben Nevis in the distance. We had looked at the churches in the town and decided to start with the Church of Scotland. Later in the holiday we would visit the 'Wee Frees', we thought, and maybe others.

There were the usual quick looks at a family of six all in the pew together. Just as the service was about to begin, the churchwarden carried a huge Bible from the vestry to the pulpit and placed it there with great reverence. If he had been a high churchman he would have kissed it. The minister was called Allan Ramsey. And we felt very much at home.

On the drive back, Jonathan gave us impressions of Allan Ramsey saying 'Welcome to Lochaber'; Allan Ramsey talking about bees, and while we were still laughing someone said,

'We'll be going there for the rest of the holiday, won't we?' So we did. The Wee Frees would have to manage without us.

The days passed in magnificence. Western Scotland was non-plussed by the heatwave that had arrived with us. People were climbing Ben Nevis in bikinis. We climbed it ourselves, decently clothed. Half-way up was my limit; I settled with the baggage and insisted on the others carrying coats and chocolate to the top. But all they needed was the mug they took, to catch water from the streams on the way. Even in that heat, there was snow on the top.

We all carried mugs on the way down, catching drinks where we could. There were no gushing torrents today, merely a few trickles in shady places.

Our last Saturday was spent at the Highland Games in Fort William. You see pictures of huge men tossing the caber against a background of mountains and I wondered if the whole day would be bleak and rugged like the pictures. Instead, we had a gala. Families had come to enjoy themselves; they had brought a bagful of sandwiches, a couple of nappies, Grandma and plenty of money for ice-creams.

We wandered off on our own errands for a bit, past the candyfloss and basketwork stalls, along by the Highland dancing, but we were all back beside the track in time for the Melantee Hill Race. The public address system was working well; the Master of Ceremonies was relaxed and efficient.

'Ladies and gentlemen, the competitors are now lining up for the Melantee Hill Race. If you look up beyond the far end of the park, you will see a hill with a radio mast at the top. That is Melantee. The competitors will complete one lap of the field and then go out of the park and up the hill. Members of the Lochaber Mountain Rescue Team are already in their places, marking the route and ready to give any assistance that may be required.'

There was still some weight-lifting and hammer throwing before the race began; it gave visitors the chance to have their cameras ready. I looked up at Melantee and imagined a stumbling, breathless run. Oh well, I thought, we shall be gone home to tea before they get back.

There were teams from Preston and Blackpool, Inverness and Tayside, along with the Lochaber team, starting off with a tremendous cheer from the crowd. When they had left the field there were other races, but our glances kept straying up the hill. Soon the steep hillside was dotted with running figures, all going as fast as if they were running on level ground.

Half an hour after the start, the ice-cream stalls and tea-bar were deserted; everyone had moved in round the track to welcome the runners back. Precisely thirty-five minutes after the race began, the first men were back in Claggan Park. They were all back within the hour.

Now the pictures on the porridge packets came to life—Tossing the Caber. This huge telegraph pole was offered to each competitor in turn but none could toss it. So up came two men with a wheel-barrow, took out their two-man saw and cut a couple of feet off the caber. It was now just possible to toss it; time and again it fell back the way it had come. A successful toss throws it on end and makes it fall away from its starting point. Finally Bob Davidson, a huge man in a red kilt, was declared the winner and the Lochaber Highland Games were over for another year.

We drove right across Scotland on our homeward morning, enjoying our last look at hills and streams, cool pine forests and sturdy towns. Over the Forth Bridge and into Edinburgh. A quick shopping trip—it was Jonathan's birthday next day—and then home on the train. British Rail was alive again.

It was one of Jonathan's birthday presents that stopped us in our tracks when we went to Belfast. We were already late for the ferry because the train had been delayed, and here we were, having our luggage searched for bombs. We had packed some presents, ready for his birthday at the end of the week. The searchers picked out a large cardboard box.

'What's in here, Jonathan?' called Christopher across the Customs shed.

'Dunno,' said Jon, relaxed as usual. 'It's my birthday present from Rosie.' It didn't seem heavy enough to contain rounds of ammunition so they waved us on.

Belfast tugs at the heart; the people are so welcoming, so determined to get on with their lives in spite of the troubles. Never a day passes but I think of Northern Ireland, even when it is not in the news. I would love to go back.

Londonderry, even more than Belfast, made us feel the sorrow of the conflict. We drove westwards in a hired car one morning, through the Sperrin Mountains and down beside the river Foyle. The towns are all quite small, the countryside wide and green. Yes, the emerald isle.

We were looking forward to visiting the Guildhall, and the brochure said there was a lot to be seen by walking along the city walls. But there had been two bombs in Ballynahinch that week and the people of Londonderry were taking no chances. The Guildhall was closed and the ancient city walls punctuated by barbed wire.

Well, at least the Cathedral will be open, we thought. We saw ourselves absorbing the atmosphere of the place where Cecil Frances Alexander wrote her hymns. But that, too, was locked and deserted.

Our next stop was an archway under the city wall, while the rain teemed down.

'Got any sweets?' said one of the boys. We pulled off our hoods and shook the rain off our shoulders and passed the sweets around.

We were not alone in the archway. There was a soldier crouching there, on the lookout; a young fellow no older than Tim.

'Would you like a Murraymint?' I asked him. He looked so weary, but he said Yes, he'd love a Murraymint and if it went on raining like this he'd get the life boat out for us. He put the sweet down on his knee and opened it with his left hand and his teeth, awkwardly. He couldn't use his right hand; it was at the ready, holding his gun.

Next door to where we were living was a Baptist family; we were friends from the start. The girls were occupied during the second week with a Scripture Union mission. All the Knockbreda churches were sharing in it. On the Friday evening they said, 'Will you come with us to a Swarm?' Marcus, finding the Ulster accent difficult to follow sometimes, looked for his swimming trunks.

But it was a code-name used on the Mission and meant a family get-together. It was down at the Presbyterian church at the other end of the village. We played energetic team games and then queued up for hamburgers and soft drinks.

And while we were queueing up, our family nearly came unstuck. Christopher, Jonathan and Jeremy between them had got hold of one of the footballs from the team games.

'Bet you couldn't kick it over the roof of the church,' said one of them.

'Bet I could,' said another. So out they went and it took so long to come over that the waiting one thought it must have got stuck on the roof. One more blocked church gutter, one more leaking roof. But at last it sailed over. Mercifully, merely one more memory of Belfast.

Coming home is always hard. Suddenly the train is running into the suburbs and then into central London. We go down into the tube and out again at Aldgate into the hot street, to wait for a bus. By Stepney East Station we see the church tower rising above all other buildings.

'George Davis is innocent' proclaims the railway bridge. It has been saying that for fifteen years. The blue paint on Cohen's old print works 'The 600 Group' is pealing off in chunks. Two of the upper windows are half open and two of the lower ones are broken. Under the next bridge and we get off, into the roar of the traffic.

There is one other time when I feel the sudden re-entry keenly and that is when we go on a parish outing to the seaside. We leave the beach in that wonderful quiet lull that seems to take over at teatime, hushing the sea, easing the wind and softening the glare of the sun.

By the time we have settled down for the journey, the coach is driving through the Kent countryside. We pass the quiet fields and farms lying there in the evening sunlight and I can hardly bear to leave them behind. Then through Sidcup and the Blackwall Tunnel and out into the roar of the A13 and the heat lingering in the streets.

When all the family are away together on holiday, we have to ask someone to live in the house to keep it safe. Several times it has been Alban who actually sleeps here, and his family drop round and join him most days.

They are long-standing church members and live in a flat nearby. One year Iris gave us a photo of Dave out in our garden in an armchair. It was captioned 'The watchman on duty!'

There is often quite a bit of August left when we return home, but with a bicycle and a cricket bat, what more can you want? I remember this zany conversation one morning before we all poured out into the road.

'Do you mind if I have the A to Z? I'm going up Bishopsgate and I'm not sure of the way.'

'Honestly Mum, even you couldn't get lost. It's a straight road.'

'Do you mind having my lock and I'll have yours?'

'Why? (This was in the days before we all bought Citadel locks.)

'Well, I'm going to the French Embassy and I don't want to cart this heavy lock all that way.' There was no answer to that one; the rest of us were going to such humble places as Marks & Spencer or St Paul's.

'I'll give you a twenty minute start, Mum,' said Marcus. Yet even I, pottering along at my own speed, can manage to cycle to Fleet Street or Holborn. We may long for the countryside but at least, being in the city, we have the great advantage of being near the centre.

One can also cycle to the Oval Cricket Ground. In our family there is County Cricket watched live, cricket on the television, family cricket in Victoria Park with a picnic tea, cricket in the churchyard and illicit cricket in the back garden.

'One of the tomato plants is broken,' I said one day. 'Could somebody pay for it? I'm not having them broken for nothing.'

'Oh but Mum, it wasn't for nothing,' said Jeremy. 'He got three runs off that ball.'

Since I married Christopher I have had a whole new education in cricket, football and athletics. The boys are very kind to me; they talk to me about it all as if I were their equal, instead of a hopelessly ignorant mother.

I still don't understand about the off-side rule, but even Jonathan, who is a qualified FA referee, finds it difficult to enforce. The important television programmes in our house are Match of the Day, Football Focus and Midweek Sports Special or Cricket, Cricket Highlights and more Cricket, depending what time of year it is.

'Mum, you've forgotten how to be a woman,' said

Marcus one day. 'All you talk about is football.' Well, look who I live with. But there are currently two delightful girlfriends loosely attached to the family, so maybe my conversation will improve.

There are often visitors to take out in the summer. Paul, a godson, wanted to see Madame Tussaud's and Oxford Street. So we joined the queue of visitors from all over the world.

Naturally the boys wanted to see the Chamber of Horrors and I didn't. So I lingered among the great while they went on and suddenly, in that hall full of captains and kings, I came upon a different King. Martin Luther King, all alone behind a pillar and the tears pricked in my eyes. He looked lonely. I wanted Hugh Latimer and Nicholas Ridley and Katharine Mompesson to step forward and keep him company. Has Madame Tussaud's no heroes to stand beside him?

We went out into the hot sunshine, along Baker Street, past the Sherlock Holmes Hotel and across to Hyde Park.

We had brought our own lunch. We always do unless it is snowing, otherwise we fall into what Jeremy calls 'The Tourist Trap'. Outside the pedestrian subway was a man selling tins of Coke, which were standing on a huge block of ice. That year you could buy them for fifteen pence at our grocer's. I fell into the Trap.

'Jeremy, here's thirty pence,' I said. 'Go and get one and we'll share it.' He came back laughing. 'He wanted sixty pence for one tin,' he said. I longed for the cooler weather. The hot streets and spaces enclosed by warm brick and concrete made me think fondly of snow.

At the end of August I had to go to Mile End Hospital. It was, on my part, simply to say 'I'm fine'; they for their part had to check that. At my first visit I was one of the first patients to be seen; a meticulous medical student wrote everything down and then he and the Registrar checked it together.

Today I was the last patient to be seen; I sat for three

hours reading a book. I had a cup of coffee and I read every notice on the wall. I went to the Ladies and I phoned Christopher to say Please have some lunch. But mostly I read the book.

I am not grumbling. We have to train doctors, else we would not have any. That takes time. Every patient that morning was seen by a medical student and then had all his facts checked by a Registrar or Consultant. New patients, as I once was, were treated as important people, and every detail was noted.

Some of them were in there for ages; many of them had to make a next appointment. I was a mere Goodbye and Thank you at the end of the line. And with that I was very content.

7

A Miss on Wednesdays

O praise God in his holiness:
praise him in the firmament of his power.
Praise him in the sound of the trumpet:
praise him upon the lute and harp.
Praise him in the cymbals and dances:
praise him upon the strings and pipe (Ps 150:1, 3, 4).

Clear blue skies and sharp mornings; release from the summer's heat and an excuse for a wood fire on Sunday nights. September! And back to school again.

I was cycling through the flats one evening and came upon a game of marbles.

'Hi, everybody!' I said.

'Hallo Miss!' they shouted back in chorus. A younger boy said, 'Cor! Is she your Miss?'

Fortunately, I parked my bike in time to hear the answer.

'Nah!' said his elder brother. 'She's only a Miss on Wednesdays.'

The Cyril Jackson Primary School is two minutes' walk down the road, between us and the river. Nobody could miss it, standing there on the corner and backed by the railway arches. It was built in the 1970s, low and pleasant, in warm brown brick.

Open the door and you are greeted by colour everywhere, the walls and ceiling covered in artwork and displays. It sometimes reminds me of 'A partridge in a pear tree' when I walk in just after the afternoon bell has rung.

Twelve in the sandtray, eleven in the water, ten infants painting, nine sewing samplers, eight pasting collage, seven in the Wendy house, six counting buttons, five playing shop. And upstairs, four Chinese playing chess, three Vietnamese sawing wood, two Asians learning tapestry and Mkungu playing top E.

At the end of 1977, the current Headmistress said to Christopher, 'Do you know anyone who wants a job? We have nobody in our school who can play any kind of music.'

I was missing my weekly stint of teaching Religious Education in our old church school in Poplar. Not so much the actual teaching, simply the junior children.

So a few days later, I was sitting in the Head's study, telling her how much I would like the job. 'I'm not very good at playing the piano,' I said, 'but I like junior children and I think singing should be fun. One finger and a lot of oomph is better than Mozart when it comes to "I'm 'Enery the eighth, I am". And I can manage more than one finger!'

'You're on,' she said. 'Four hours a week.' So I became a Miss on Tuesdays, changing to Wednesdays two years ago. It was a pushover in those far off days. I used to arrive, sit at the piano and wait for the teachers to bring their classes in. I played the first line of each appointed song and away we went.

Soon Easter was looming and the teachers were trying to introduce some Easter hymns.

'You're not singing that right; it goes up at the end,' they would say. Which had me on my feet.

'Would it be easier if I sang it to them?' We learnt an Easter Round and singing became fun.

One afternoon early in the term I heard music coming from the hall during playtime and couldn't resist going to see who and what. There were half a dozen girls, forlornly playing recorders, three of them with their right hand at the top instead of their left. They had begun to learn but now there was no-one to teach them.

'See you next week, same time, same place,' I said. So every week I went to the hall with my mug of tea and we had an informal class during playtime. The Head found some school recorder books in her cupboard and we made strides.

During the summer term, she called me into her study.

'You will stay, won't you?' she said. Wild horses wouldn't have dragged me away.

'Now, would you be willing to work for five hours a week? I'd like you to teach recorders more formally and have some beginners' groups.'

I am surprised, looking back, at how seriously I had to think this over before I said Yes. I didn't want to become a 'working wife' and adding an hour a week seemed to bring this dire fate nearer. I agreed, of course, and from then on the job evolved over the years. There are other musicians in the school now who take singing. So for over a year, I have spent the whole day teaching children to play the recorder.

The beginning of every term is always busy with a whole new crop of learners. I work well over five hours a week and then find it compensated towards the end of term when classes are away on visits or school journeys.

Top infants are always wide-eyed at their first meeting with a recorder and thrilled to play their first note. By week three, they have either decided they like it, or are deeply disillusioned that they cannot yet play every tune in the world.

'Why don't you have a break and come back after the next holiday?' I say. So half the new ones disappear overnight, but the ones who come for the second time round usually settle down and make a good job of it.

Most years I have the privilege of teaching someone who began on page one like everybody else and can now play better than I can. This is a peak of joy.

Walking into the staffroom on Wednesday morning is always a relaxed moment. They sit there drinking coffee and swapping funny stories, but look into any classroom and the day's work is all set out ready. I go on up to 'my' room—the music room, tucked away at the top of the stairs.

It still feels like a treat to work up there. For several years we had recorder classes in the medical room; a quiet haven for most of the time, though you never knew when one of the helpers would come in, leading someone with a nose-bleed or a cut knee. First-aid among the music stands could be a bit off-putting to the musicians.

I dreaded the days when the school nurse appeared and we had to find a corner of the library area near the front door. What with plates and saucepans clattering in the kitchen before dinner and the general activity all around us in the afternoons, concentration was hard to come by. Michael's 'Cor Miss, it ain' arf noisy, ain' it?' summed up our feelings exactly.

But now, with some rearrangement of classes and activities, the music room houses all the percussion instruments, the guitars and the recorders. On the door, the timetable reads 'Wednesdays—Marjorie'. I shove the tables around and put everything ready. Another Wednesday has begun.

'You've spelt my name wrong, Miss,' says Suad. We spell all the Asian names phonetically but I have slipped up this time. She helps me give out letters to the group, which say that children can buy a recorder at school for £1.50. But even buying one does not guarantee loving care. The most conscientious children can treat their recorders unkindly; they wander through the school carrying the poor thing naked, bumping it against doorways.

'Next time you bring it to class without its cover, I shall send you away again,' I say. And I do.

'Linda, I know you've lost the cover but can't your

Mum make one out of some old pyjamas?' She never did, so I made a few spares—out of old pyjamas.

Farzana's brother broke her recorder in half, (how?), Shahida's younger sister poured nail varnish over hers and Donna's mother spring-cleaned twice but couldn't find the missing treasure. I'd hate to be a recorder at Cyril Jackson school!

At break time I am first in the staff room and settle down with a magazine all about computers in primary schools. John comes in and explains how he would want to use a computer for teaching; a child would be able to discover if the leaf he was holding was an oak leaf or a chestnut leaf.

'And what will this do for the children of Cyril Jackson?' I ask. 'Widen their horizons or merely teach them how to use a computer?'

'Widen their horizons, definitely,' says John.

I wonder, as I munch my marmalade and toast sandwich. John is an experienced teacher. But doesn't a week away in Essex at the Field Study centre teach them even more? And cost less?

Ann comes in giggling.

'You know that very bright new boy I've got? I was asking general knowledge questions all round and then I let them ask some. His was—What was the name of the first Pharoah? Imagine!' We all laugh and sympathise.

'Like me to pick him up for recorders?' I say. 'Give him something to get his teeth into. It's not too late in the term to start him off.'

Five more minutes to sip coffee. Kate and Grace are talking about Mrs Peppermint, who is about to produce another child. Five have already passed through the school and after a gap, there are now two more enjoying life in the infants' department. 'She says she just loves babies. And she keeps the place spotless. . . .'

At the other end of the room Minu, wearing her green sari shot with blue, is discussing arranged marriages.

'. . . so how do you think they feel? They cannot talk to each other alone; always the family is there. And if they go to the pictures, the brothers and sisters and the aunt, they come too. Then suddenly, they are married. The sleeping, the washing, going to the toilet, everything . . . they are alone together. It is terrifying. . . .'

Anne is still munching a plateful of Weetabix.

There is a knock at the door; Le Minh stands there, smiling the friendly smile of the six-year-old whose new front teeth have not quite arrived.

'Miss Mcleod says she's ringing the bell in one minute.' So we scatter.

Like any other job, there are times when it seems a grind. But if I think it's a grind, what do the learners think? I try to change gear, do a bit of percussion or half a minute of theory, or go right back to page 3 to boost their confidence. Then I turn them out before their fifteen minutes are up. The next group will be different and I relax. After one particularly slow-learning but dogged group, I have some older juniors. They come bursting in, eager to begin, and tick me off.

'Don't you remember Miss? You said we'd be on for 'Down in Demarara' this week.'

I count them in 'One, two, D, G . . .' and away they go, enjoying themselves. Take a slice of the school anywhere and you would come up with a similar group to this one.

Brian is thin-faced and threadbare at the knees. He has shrewd eyes and a real East London grin. Winston is a gentle giant of a West Indian, with the most curly eyelashes you ever saw. Ayaz looks like a fat, prosperous merchant from the Middle East but like half our school population he comes from Bangladesh. Many of them are only nominal Muslims but Ayaz's family are devout and faithful; they leave their shoes in the hall when they get home. Smita is also Asian but her family are a rarity round here; they are Indian and Hindus. All the children live and work happily together, passing on the tradition of helping one another which makes our school a good place to be.

The Demarara gang leave and Natalie comes in with Farzana.

'There's a lunch-hour concert on in two week's time. I thought you might enjoy it. Would you like to go?' They are my two best recorder players and a live concert will give them some stimulus. We chat about wind instruments and I promise to fix it with the Head and their mothers.

The afternoon follows the same pattern and suddenly there is a joyful moment. The group has at last mastered top E and a whole new world is open to them. The National Anthem, 'The Bluebells of Scotland' and a hundred other well-known tunes lie within their grasp. By Christmas they should be able to manage 'Hark, the herald angels sing'!

September brings our church anniversary. The building was finished during the late 1720s and then stood empty while 'certain difficulties'—money, of course, and power—were overcome. Finally it was opened and consecrated on September 12th, 1730.

Come 1980, it was time to celebrate two hundred and fifty years. The first thing we did was to borrow a huge yellow banner saying '250th Anniversary' from Christ Church Spitalfields. They are a year older than us.

And so, one blustery February afternoon, when our boys were on half-term but not the juniors, a boy in the top class at Stepney Greencoat School looked out of the window and said, 'Sir, Sir, look!' Sir was not the only one to obey the call. Beyond the flats and the tyre dealer, straight across from the first-floor classroom window, rose the tower of the parish church and up there on the pinnacles were three figures.

'Sir, Sir, what are they doing Sir? Won't they fall off?' The whole class was at the windows now and Sir thought he might as well take it from there.

'You can all watch carefully and then draw what you've seen.'

So on the following Wednesday morning Christopher was invited to see the drawings of himself, Timothy and Jonathan fixing the banner to the pinnacles of the tower.

As usual, he hadn't told me what they were doing until they had done it. I always worry when they are up to something above roof level.

The Anniversary year gave us an excuse for doing unusual things. A neighbour brought a few friends to sing Evensong. The previous Rector came back to preach. Cyril Jackson school choir and recorders came to enhance Evening Prayer.

And we had a grand Sale of Work when it poured with rain—the sort of day when you count the hours until bed-time.

> 'Towering over road and river
> stands this house of prayer . . .'

we sang in May, when the orchestra from All Souls', Langham Place visited us. It goes to the tune of 'Angel voices ever singing' and Christopher wrote it for our Anniversary year. We could do with singing it more often.

Our main celebration was the Service on September 12th. I was breathless with tension for most of the service, particularly as the orchestral music, conducted by me, did not go all that well. But Michael Gillingham played the organ, Bishop Maurice Wood preached and the school choir sang, 'Freedom train' and 'Steal away to Jesus'.

These are the things to remember.

Then there was before and after. Before, I went across to the carpark behind the church with an overall covering my finery, to pick up the last pieces of broken glass left by the alcoholics. The whole family was working flat out and Christopher had already spent a lot of time on the glass; I was putting the last touches. Quite a peaceful job, out there in the evening sunlight.

Just as I had finished, a messenger—Jeremy I think—came to tell me that the principal guest of the evening had arrived. I came back carrying this bucket of broken glass and greeted the Bishop of Norwich as he stepped out of his car, in his purple cassock.

He said, 'Can I come over and help you finish?' and if there had been some more to do I would have said, 'Yes please!' He had been a Vicar in Islington and used to get dead rats thrown over his garden wall.

Afterwards, we entertained our many visitors upstairs in the gallery with tea and cakes. Norry McCurry, the Area Dean, made a short speech.

'When this church needed a Rector, I knew that nobody in his right mind would take it on. Then Chris Idle said he would do it. . . .' While we were all laughing, there was a rumble downstairs. When we went down later, we found large chunks of ceiling plaster lying on the floor near the font. The tramping of so many feet overhead had been too much for it. There was rather a lot; mercifully nobody had been underneath it.

One year, the 12th was a Sunday and we used it as a Day of Prayer and Giving; the church was open all afternoon for members or visitors to go in and pray. It was a peaceful afternoon; the family took turns to be in church and keep an eye on things, with Christopher doing the lion's share. Janet took a turn too; she was living with us and working in the parish for a month.

At teatime Christopher said to me, 'Would you do the second reading in church this evening?' It was on the tip of my tongue to say, 'As long as there's nothing about fire in it.' What made me think of such a thing at that moment? Only that year in July, I had sobbed my way through a chapter about fire and destruction in the weekday Morning Prayer; and to this day, I cannot manage Psalm 74. Sternly I told myself not to trifle with old fears.

'Yes of course,' I said. And the doorbell rang.

'Is this the Reverend's house? Someone's set light to the church door. The one round the back, like.' Christopher was running down the steps with the man before I had finished saying ' . . . south porch'. The boys and Janet rose as one man, collected water from the kitchen and went out. I phoned the fire brigade.

It was a very small fire, just a couple of smouldering rags. But we were shaken. No wonder Christopher wrote,

> 'Wars may rage, and fire and trouble;
> still your people stand:
> love divine is measured double,
> faith and hope regained:
> we are tried, but not forsaken,
> never shaken from your hand.'

8

Autumn

Let the people praise thee, O God:
  let all the people praise thee.
Then shall the earth bring forth her increase:
  and God, even our own God, shall give us his blessing
(Ps 67:5, 6).

Our street was built before planning was invented. Two smart new houses with low tiled roofs, built on an old stable block, stand cheek by jowl with corrugated iron enclosing a wasteland. Our house faces a much larger one built by Nelson for Lady Hamilton, while on our right stands a renovated block of flats. Walk down the street past the houses built in Dickens' time and you find modern council flats that make our part of East London look just like every other part.

But the piece of our street that interests me at Festival times is the waste ground opposite. There, Nature has a few square yards to herself, lush and green. From the first hint of pussy-willow to the last yellow leaf of autumn, there are rich pickings here for all who decorate the church. Harvest Saturday brought early morning rain streaming against the windows. I put on wellingtons and, gritting my teeth, went across the street with secateurs and a big cardboard box.

I needed enough greenery to decorate each window-sill, as a background to the oranges and apples we would put there. This plot was a cottage garden, in the days when our street was called Church Row. There was a clump of golden rod in the corner; I brushed past dripping bushes and gathered an armful. A couple of local dogs came bounding up to me, swishing raindrops round my ankles with every movement. We passed the time of day and they rushed off, showering me once more.

Only a few people come to church with their gifts on the Saturday, not enough to make a good display. Most prefer to bring them on Sunday morning. We have a procession during the first hymn when all the gifts are brought to the front, much enjoyed by the children. So I had bought apples and oranges the day before, ready for the window-sills.

Mike and Jonathan arrived with their recorders while I was working. We went up to the gallery together, sorted out the music and decided where to put our music stands. Then we tuned our recorders with the organ.

First there was 'Come, ye thankful people come' with recorder and organ, moving to recorders only for the middle verses. Then later came,

> 'For the fruits of his creation
> Thanks be to God'

sung to the tune of 'All through the night'. One of the warmest marriages of new words and old tune that I know.

At lunchtime I remembered to take the harvest loaf out of the freezer and that evening we put it on the Communion table with a bunch of grapes from Winnie, her gift every year.

Sunday was a good day; families came to church with fruit and groceries, strangers came, attracted by our invitations. A whole friendly gang of children whom I teach in school crowded into the back row.

Thou crownest the year with thy goodness. . . .
The folds shall be full of sheep;
  the valleys also shall stand so
  thick with corn that they shall
  laugh and sing (Ps 65:12, 14).

Harvest Monday always keeps me busy. After sparing a mere fragment of time for sock-washing and bed-making, I went over to church with a large cardboard box. It only took a few minutes to dismantle the window-sill displays and bring everything to the front of the church. Christopher and I worked together stacking and sorting.

'There's forty packets of tea and seventeen bags of sugar,' I said. 'Who would like this enormous cabbage? Oh, we must put a nice packet of biscuits on one side for George.'

We spread our name labels on the floor and made up a bag of fruit and groceries for every name. There was a little left over and we piled it into a box. During the next two days we should suddenly think of people who ought to be on the list; it would all be used up by the end of the week.

I took a small bagful of things home with me—bits that were not exactly what every senior citizen had been waiting for. There was a head of celery that had grown tired of life, a rotting apple and a squashed peach. There was also the bunch of grapes off the Communion table.

'These aren't to go round the parish on Monday,' Winnie had said. 'They're for your family to enjoy.'

After lunch we began our visits. Some of the gifts would be taken by other church members, but Christopher and I do a lot of the nearby ones. I went to Mary first; she was eighty and used to be a district nurse. Scared of lifts, I walked up the four flights, pausing on the third floor to draw breath and look out over the river, just a hundred yards away.

A police launch came chugging up Limehouse Reach, making for base at Wapping; a tug pulling three barges went down towards Greenwich. Apart from them, the river was empty, like a deserted High Street.

Breathing more comfortably after the pause, I went on up to Mary. She beamed at me as she took the bag.

'Oh, you are good to me,' she said. 'Will you have a cup of tea?'

'No, thank you. I've got lots to deliver this afternoon. Is Mrs Littlemore with you?' She was, so I went in for a minute to hand over her gift. Herbert had just finished cleaning the windows, so I delved in my large bag and with a little rearrangement, found I had something for him too. When I first met him he was Bert, but since Mary called him Herbert, I have followed suit ever since.

These three used to look after each other just the way people did when there were little streets with houses, even though they now lived in a tower block. Only Herbert is left but he manages to enjoy life with help from the Day Centre for the handicapped and the Psychiatric Rehabilitation Association. In spite of the rather grand name, this is a friendly club that meets once a week.

Mrs Littlemore was forgetful and lonely, so she would come to Mary some afternoons. Herbert took to cleaning her windows too, and sometimes she would remember to buy him and Mary something nice for tea.

Mary had been here for years, cycling defiantly round Docklands during the war and after. She had been a neighbour of Herbert's when he was a boy, and here she was at the last, a good neighbour to him still. She would remind him to pay the rent or buy new clothes, mind his money if he was saving up for new shoes, and cook him an evening meal three times a week.

He would do the shopping and have Mary up in his flat twice a week to give her a change of scenery.

It was Mary who told me Mrs Littlemore had died in an asthma attack, and Herbert who called to tell me Mary had been taken ill.

'Nurse is in hospital. Mile End she's in. I'm going up there to see her termorrer.'

So each year we take a few names off our Harvest list and add others.

Is it just a chore, a habit the church has got into, taking all this greengrocery around? Or a hark-back to Lady Bountiful going round the village with the soup-can?

No; it's an excuse for a visit, the actual gifts are always welcome and often the recipients give more than they receive.

One year we thought it would be a good idea to take David round the sheltered housing opposite, doing the Harvest visits. He had been a recluse for some years and now he was just beginning to come to church and hope that people would talk to him. They did.

So we set off across the churchyard, David coaxing my huge pushalong basket over the flagstones. It was full to the brim with goodies.

'I'm the brawn and you're the brains,' he said. 'Don't suppose anyone will speak to me, though.' Just as Eeyore might have done.

Instead, he spent an hour knocking on doors and handing tins to all those sweet elderly residents. They gave him beaming smiles and thanked him warmly. They melted his heart so much that he began to come to the monthly service we hold in the big sitting room over there. I could have hugged them all.

And there was that embarrassing morning, back in Poplar, when Jonathan and Marcus fancied themselves as Father Christmas. They must have been about nine and four years old and they wanted to help distribute the gifts. So we gave them parcels for four pensioners who we knew would be glad to see them, and sent them off. They were away longer than we expected; we ought to have foreseen what would happen but we didn't.

'Lovely boys, Mr. Idle. It was really nice to have them.' They were entertained royally in each household and came home bursting with orange juice and cake. And their pockets were full of money, some for the church and most of it for themselves!

Running with Harvest and finished by the time the clocks go back, we have a Monday Club for the Explorers. With a limit on free evenings, since all the leaders have other jobs in the church as well, we could never keep going throughout the year. But there is nothing to stop us finding four or five evenings in spring and autumn when we can run a club.

We have it in our house, because our kitchen is easier to work in when there are four people making biscuits at the same time. There is nothing like a warm carpet to sit on, either, for playing Pairs or Jack Straws.

I can never believe how quiet Club Night is. Being in someone else's house, playing someone else's games, is totally absorbing. I would never have thought that Draughts and a Model Garden and a Fuzzy-felt could keep my gang of seven to ten year olds so enthralled.

What about the mess in the kitchen after cooking biscuits? Was it worth it, I asked myself one year. I was put right when Jenny came and flung herself round me as I came out of the school gate one day.

'Miss, when can I come and cook biscuits like my brother?'

'Well,' I said, 'when are you going up into the juniors?'

'Next summer, Miss.'

'Seems like an awful long time to wait, doesn't it? But I promise we'll still be having Club and we'll cook biscuits.' She nodded, her silent self again and we smiled Goodbye.

So cooking biscuits is important. I make the dough earlier in the day. The beauty of it, you understand, is not in struggling to make the dough but in cutting out the shapes and eating the results later.

Four round the kitchen table is quite possible, with two milk bottles standing in as rolling pins and two real ones. And an assortment of cutters—stars and hearts as well as circles.

While Alison and Ian get beaten at Draughts and absolutely mown down at Pairs, I preside over the oven and coax everyone to get their baking tray into it by twenty to seven.

We join the others in the sitting room, still a bit floury, and in no time it is five to seven. Orange squash, a goodnight prayer and bags of warm biscuits for the cooks to take home.

Two days after our own Harvest, it was school Harvest Festival at Stepney Greencoat. There was a magnificant display of fruit, vegetables and tins, carefully built by two of the teachers.

Children sat on the floor at the front, parents and visitors on chairs at the back, while the autumn sun poured through the windows. I thought of the hot summer afternoon when we first came to see the school, looking for the right place for Jeremy and Marcus. There had been a comfortable, happy feeling about the school, in spite of the intense heat of 1976, and in every class people were busy at work. Peter, the Head, had enthused about his staff.

'We've got stability without stagnation,' he said, in his strong Dorset accent.

Today there was the same happy atmosphere. Christopher enlivened his Bible talk with some giant pictures of Mr Greedy and friends, which we had carted up Salmon Lane with some difficulty in the breeze.

Next day it was Harvest Festival at my school, Cyril Jackson. It was a celebration of food, with thankfulness, but more to the mothers who cooked it than to God who gave it. Christopher was invited and the Head allowed him to say a Prayer of Thanks; but he must not ask the children to join in or to say Amen.

The Head's policy is that we must be careful not to give offence in a school where over half the children are not English and nearly half are Muslims. So the Christian content of the Festival was rather meagre, though the choir, bless them, had made their own free choice of songs to sing—'Lord of the autumn gold' from David Mowbray's hymn 'Lord of the changing year'; and 'Come sing praises to the Lord above'.

Our mouths were watering by the end; in addition to another magnificent display of provisions, there were samples of special food prepared by the children—chapatis and rye bread, rolls and waffles, pizzas and matzos. Yes, there is a busy, happy atmosphere at my school too, but the Lord Jesus Christ is not a common subject of conversation there, as he is up the road, and so they lose out on a whole dimension.

There was coffee afterwards for any visitors brave enough to join the informality of the staffroom at playtime. We made a beeline for a seasoned Governor, Mrs Eva Armsby, who had been Mayor one year.

'Lovely to hear the children singing,' she said in her disarmingly soft Welsh voice. 'And I'm glad you said that prayer. Keep it up.' She is on the local council, a staunch campaigner for pensioners' rights and a staunch Christian too.

A few days later I found myself, breathless, on a coach heading for Canterbury. I was having my Solitary Break.

When Christopher first packed me off for a break, we did not realise what a brilliant idea it was. Now, we each go every year. I have climbed the hills above Chichester, wrestling with problems and finding by the time I reached the top that they were in some sort of perspective again. Climbing the Downs, or sitting by the sea at high tide, watching the water in the brilliant winter sunlight, or sitting by Wynne's gas fire in the evening—these have been my times to breathe deeply and then go on again.

Christopher, too, likes to go on solitary walks, shedding the pressures and feeling the wind on his face.

I can hear someone saying—Oh, but surely you ought to take breaks together, not separately. Yes, we have been able to do that too, since the boys got old enough to be left at home on their own. But the solitary break is still important.

Sitting on the coach as we sped out of London, I had mixed feelings. A warm nostalgia at passing through my home town again—there's Danson Park Lido, there's the end of Arbuthnot Lane—and a sadness at the wide swathe of new road cutting through the old familiar territory.

I used to cycle down Arbuthnot Lane as a young teenager, bearing the family's Ration Books. Straight across the dual carriageway as it was then, scarcely a car in sight, and then on down the second half of the same lane to the Food Office, where our surplus Bread Units could be changed into Points. Points would buy tins of fruit.

We swept past Bexley and up on to Dartford Heath. Just north of the road was my old school. Southwards lay the winding road through the Darent valley to Sevenoaks. A group of friends, a bicycle and a packed lunch—what more could a teenager want on a long summer's day?

We would linger by the ford at Eynsford and then go on to Shoreham, with its memorial cross cut into the chalk hillside like the Long Man of Wilmington. Maybe we would go home up Farthing Lane, turning back for a view across the valley. If we were lucky there was a glimpse of a coastbound steam train on the viaduct. Then we would make for Crockenhill and the Cray valley, homewards.

On a good day we might be more energetic, cycle as far as Sevenoaks and then go home up Polhill. Just the name conjures up a picture of the Weald of Kent, stretching away in the haze to Tonbridge, Goudhurst and the hopfields. And there is the road itself. The A21 climbs up out of the valley in a long curve, from bottom to top of Polhill. It is built on the very edge of the hill so, assuming you haven't got seventeen gears on your bike, you walk up with the cliff overhanging you. But the eastern edge of the road drops away, down the escarpment, giving a panoramic view across the Darent valley to the hills beyond, the villages lying there in the warm sunshine and all the quiet fields and farms at evening.

The mountains are majestic, the sea is fun; but always, Kent is where I would like to be. Just for once, I was.

Motorways have changed the way we travel; there used to be a stop for coffee on the way down but today we were bypassing Rochester and speeding towards Faversham without so much as changing gear.

Canterbury was as beautiful as ever, in the October sunshine. The cathedral was still there—I had seen it as we came in. But was Dane John still there? I checked the time of my bus out to Bramling and then crossed the road. There it was, just as I always see it in my affectionate daydreams, ankle-deep in leaves, children and dogs running in delight down the slope and scuffling in the leaves at the bottom, the trees casting long shadows under the autumn sky.

I walked up the slope and on to the old city wall; little groups of office workers and late tourists were having a lunch-time stroll up there. I walked slowly, pleasurably up the mound, round and round to the top. A tall stone stands on the summit. I used to think it was a memorial to Dane John, whoever he was, but if you read the inscription you find that the worthy citizens put it up as a memorial to themselves in the nineteenth century. I came down again content that here, at least, nothing had changed in the years since I was a midwife here, in Canterbury.

Among the trees, on a Victorian bench, I lingered over my flask of coffee and cheese roll, unwilling to cut short the moment, reluctant to leave the peace of this specially favourite place of mine. 'Come on,' I told myself, 'Two lovely days ahead. Tear yourself away.'

I was going to stay with Kathleen and Rhoda, who

run a small conference centre in the countryside. They had been our friends for years and it was time I visited them again.

The Deal bus put me down at Bramling and I strolled along the lane. The high fields of cabbages gave way to cottage gardens and here I was, walking in through the door of the bungalow. Rhoda and Kathleen were both talking at once.

'You'll have a cup of tea, won't you? And how's our little Twinkletoes? Taller than you, probably? There's such a lot to tell you dear. The Lord has been so good to us.'

When they first moved here, before the Conference Centre was established, Kathleen worked as secretary to Lord Hawarden up at the Manor house in the village. A friend was telling us all their news and how they were finding life quite a struggle. 'But the Lord has been very good to them,' she said. 'And so has his wife.'

What bliss to go to sleep in the total silence of the Kentish night, waking lazily to get my own breakfast when I chose. I walked among the oast houses and the bare brown fields; I leaned on gates and listened to larks singing; I knelt in Ickham church and resolved to do less house-cleaning and more writing.

Then I came home and found them all well, except that one of the boys had been sick on the bus coming home from school. Wanting to be as tidy about it as possible, he had been sick into the plastic bag which contained his football kit. Oh well, I didn't resolve to do less washing, did I?

9

A week in the city

Man goeth forth to his work, and to his labour:
  until the evening.
O Lord, how manifold are thy works:
  in wisdom thou hast made them all;
  the earth is full of thy riches (Ps 104:23, 24).

If you want to do something to hit the headlines, there is not much mileage in washing socks and ironing shirts. Nor was there in half a lifetime spent planing yokes for oxen and fashioning cradles for the newly-weds of Nazareth.

The excitements are quickly over; the routine is there week after week, giving a blessed stability to a busy life. November is a quiet month, a kind of convalescence between Harvest and Christmas. There is time to make the Christmas cake and the mincemeat without having ten other things to do on the same day; and there are quiet afternoons for writing letters, ready for putting in with the cards next month. The week's work falls into place without the interruptions of Bank Holidays, snowfall or drought.

Occasionally I go and speak at a Women's Meeting on a Monday afternoon. At Trinity Methodist Church I see my old Poplar friends and they ask after the boys, finding it difficult to forget their first acquaintance with two juniors and two in the pushchair.

At Latimer Congregational Church they like me to do everything—lead the meeting, play the piano and give the address. But in a small group of ten or twelve that is not too taxing.

I began one meeting by saying, 'It's lovely to see you again. I feel that we're old friends now.'

'I ain't seen 'er before,' said a small lady in the front row.

'Oh Ada, course you 'ave,' said her neighbour. 'It's Mrs Idle.'

'No,' growled the small lady. 'I ain't seen 'er before. And that's that.'

'Well, it's lovely to see you, whether it's the first time or the tenth time,' I said. 'Let's begin with a hymn of praise. . . .' I hoped that the wheels would turn smoothly now, but my fierce friend in the front had one more spanner to throw in the works.

We came to chorus time and most people called out a number.

'Three four five,' growled the small lady.

'Right,' I said. 'The next chorus is number three hundred and forty five. Hang on . . . there are only a hundred and fifty in the book.'

'Oh, sorry Mrs Idle,' piped up one of the others. 'She means number three, then we sing the next two after, four and five, like.' Mollified, the lady gave her voice a rest and my talk was uninterrupted.

I find it quite difficult to prepare a talk for a women's meeting. Some people just go for the company—a cup of tea and a friendly chat in a warm place. Who can blame them, now that the little streets have gone and most people live in flats where few neighbours pass the door. One or two of them will fall asleep. I am not there to keep them awake at all costs; they can get a conjuror for that.

Some are reaching out to God but don't want to get too close yet; they need encouragement. And others are faithful Christians and church members, always there and glad of new light or a fresh approach to a Bible passage. I can only pray and go ahead with a subject that seems right.

I have taken a postcard of our church to three different meetings, just to wake them up. They hardly need the picture—which Christopher's brother took, clambering around where he wasn't supposed to be—since they can see the real thing from every corner of the borough.

On the back of the card it says, predictably,

> Limehouse Parish Church (St Anne's)
> London E14
> Designed by Nicholas Hawksmoor
> Consecrated 1730

and underneath that it says, 'The name of the LORD is a strong tower.' I hold the card up, read what it says and then say, 'And can you guess which part of the Bible that verse comes from?' Hands shoot up all over the room.

'Psalms,' says everyone.

'That's just what I thought,' I tell them, 'and we're all wrong! It comes from Proverbs chapter eighteen.' We all have a chuckle and then I launch into the talk proper, but I still have a few questions up my sleeve. The crossfire of discussion is as lively as in my Sunday morning Explorers and good for me as well as them.

If there is no meeting I may well go visiting.

'Come in Marjorie. Nice to see you. Molly was on the phone yesterday and she said Chris went to see her last Tuesday. I said to her, he didn't come and see *me*.' I followed Alice into her bedroom; she was getting more frail, I thought.

'Well, he can't visit everyone when he comes to Poplar,' I said, as mildly as I could, but feeling very cross inside. 'He hasn't seen Molly for ages.' You can't stop those two from comparing notes, whether it be a Harvest visit or a snow-bound, 'see if they are managing' visit; and the tragedy is, either of them could actually come to church if she chose.

It is more rewarding to visit the truly housebound, or one of the Explorers with chickenpox.

When the boys were small I read the biography of Christopher Chavasse, our old bishop of Rochester, and his brother. ('The Chavasse Twins' by Canon Selwyn Gummer). In it was a sentence I have never forgotten. Describing the home in which the future bishop grew up, when his father, too, was a bishop, it said, 'The afternoons were spent in visiting—Mrs Chavasse on her round of calls and the Bishop on his.' I stopped there for a long time. How? I asked myself. Every afternoon out visiting? when did she do the shopping, get the tea ready, catch up on all the jobs she had been interrupted in that morning?

The answer was in the previous paragraph but I was too taken aback to see it at first—servants! There were two governesses for a start, and the next sentence read, 'Sometimes one or other of the girls would ride with Mother and wait in the buggy while she made her calls.' Doubtless a servant held the reins and watched over the girls, while back home, other servants did the housework and prepared tea.

I admit to having my faithful Mrs Murphy for two hours every Tuesday; she loves the jobs I hate and keeps us dusted and polished. But how could I talk about the difficulties of bringing up children if Christopher and I had never had to do the actual work ourselves?

For a year, yes, three hundred and sixty four days to be precise, I had four children under seven to take a mile to church. Unaided, as Christopher had to be there earlier than me on a Sunday morning. So I know it can be done, and the dinner left in the oven too. Sometimes I meet mothers who say it can't. I do sympathise, but it is always what you want to do most that you manage to do.

I want to pause here and mention Eva Davis, our

vicar's wife in Peckham when Christopher was a curate there. On our first Sunday in the parish, a day of such torrential rain that Lewisham was flooded, I was struggling to waterproof three small boys ready for the walk to church. The doorbell rang and I groaned. But there stood Eva. She had brought up four boys and a girl.

'Just thought I'd walk along with you as it's your first morning,' she said, beaming at us all. She came inside and took in the situation at a glance.

'Come along Jonathan,' she said. Obediently he came. And for the next three years he came. He even ate greens for Eva.

I hope I never forget what it was like to have small children; whenever I have a church toddler for the morning, or find one on my lap in church, it's a way of saying thank you for all that Eva did for me.

Wednesday begins with Morning Prayer at seven-thirty. Christopher is there most days except Thursday and Sunday. Over the years a succession of people have joined him, from a slightly dotty graduate with a dog to a diplomat living in Narrow Street who was there every week when he was in residence. Often there is just Christopher, but I enjoy being there on Wednesdays.

Go into church in high summer and the early sun, shining straight through the east window, is a delight. The deep reds and blues of Mr Clutterbuck's stained glass glow like jewels in the full sunlight. It is a treat that the Sunday morning worshippers, not coming until ten-thirty, miss.

On a winter's morning it takes more of an effort to be there, but the refreshment to the spirit of saying the Te Deum or the Benedicite is always worth it.

> O all ye works of the Lord, bless ye the Lord,
> Praise him and magnify him for ever.

In spite of taking Assembly at Stepney Greencoat on

Wednesdays, Christopher insists on doing the breakfast washing up and I go lightly down the road to school.

Just a minute, was I wearing this blouse last week? No, it was the pink one, so all's well. In my first term at Cyril Jackson I wore a neat blue dress each week; it was simply my school uniform. When the weather turned warmer, I went in something different one day and was stopped in my tracks by six year old Rashida.

'Oh Miss,' she said, her voice registering delight and motherly concern, 'you've got new clothes. Isn't that nice?'

Down the street saying Good Morning to neighbours, under the railway bridge and round the corner.

'Hallo Miss—oh, I've forgotten my recorder.'

'Never mind,' I say, 'you can borrow one today. But next Tuesday night—clean socks and recorder, ready for the morning.'

I pour my weekly contribution of egg boxes, cornflakes cartons and yoghurt pots into the huge junk box and go to see if anything special is happening today. There is a white board on the staffroom door and all outings and visitors are written up on it.

'Maggie sick, Gillian covering, John to Bethnal Green Museum. Peter out with Chess Club lunchtime,' it says. Nothing to disturb my routine today, then. Grace catches me as I take my coat off; she and Anne would like to bring a group of infants to look inside the church and draw the windows. They are doing a project on buildings, particularly windows. Friday would probably do nicely. I promise to check with Christopher.

And so the school day begins. My objective—another page turned and worked through for each group that comes, whatever stage they are at. I only have four or six in each group, otherwise it is difficult to keep tabs on them. Sometimes in a larger group, slow learners can bluff their way through a session, giving every appearance of understanding the music. I want to be sure they do.

The windows look westward; the morning sun lights up the Nat West building and the spire of St Mary's church, Cable Street. Then a heavy shower sweeps down and the skyline ends abruptly, halfway to Stepney, as if the tower blocks in the City never existed.

By the end of the afternoon I am quite sleepy, after sitting down for much of the day. I wish the walk home were a little longer, as I adjust from school to home again.

On a Wednesday evening, once a month, we go across the churchyard to the sheltered flats—John Lawder House—and have a service in their big communal sitting-room. We are the guests; one of the residents unlocks the room, turns the heat on and opens the piano; then we come and take the service. Maybe eight church members and ten residents. Then the more sprightly ones bustle off downstairs to the dining-room and make cups of tea for all.

It would be easy and pleasant to stay and talk for half the evening but Wednesday is 'Prayer meeting night.'

I love the bit in 'Jungle Pilot' where Sam Saint, quite small, is walking along the road one evening. (His brother was later martyred in Ecuador as a missionary pilot.) His aunt meets him and says. 'Where are you going, Sam?' and he replies,

'To prayer-meeting, darn it!'[1]

I wondered if I would feel like that when we made our change-over from one large group to small ones. We used to meet all together in the rectory; I would look around the room and think—eight o'clock and all's well. Here we are, gathered together to strengthen and encourage each other. We would study the Bible until nine, then share our news and pray for each other and the world.

How could it possibly be as good when May 1985

[1] *Jungle Pilot* by Russell T Hitt (Hodder & Stoughton: London, 1960).

arrived and we split into four Home Groups? We all dislike change and I was dreading it. Well, I was wrong.

We still study the Bible, still pray for the church and the world, but gradually as the eight of us in our group have got to know each other better, we have found we are praying for each other every day. If one member is missing, he or she is prayed for particularly, whereas if one member from a group of twenty is missing, only a few people notice. There is more time to share personal news—not that we have a long gossip session; but in a small group you can ask for two matters to be prayed about instead of feeling that you must keep it to only one.

It was Helen and David who started us off on the small group idea. They were home from Indonesia, sharing their lives with us for a few months, (though the nearest house we could find them was up at Bethnal Green).

Helen belonged to our church when we came to Poplar. She was a teacher, thinking about going abroad as a missionary. A couple of young men sought her hand, but she was waiting for the Prince. And then, one September day, six years after saying goodbye to him, she had a letter saying he would be in London on Monday. . . .

Ten months later they were married, and the year after, they went to Indonesia with the Overseas Missionary Fellowship. They have been 'our' missionaries ever since, and to have them actually sharing the life and work of the parish for eight months was a tremendous bonus.

Henry, who is in our Home Group, never forgets them; every Wednesday he mentions them.

'We should pray for the Hazlewoods, shouldn't we?' His soft Irish voice is always a little hesitant but his resolve to remember them is unshakeable.

One Wednesday there were only three of us in the group and so there was quite a lot for each of us to pray for. In a long silence I nudged Henry, 'Would you pray for the Hazlewood children?' I said. So he prayed for Anna and Thomas and Naomi '. . . and little John . . .' he said as if he were holding him on his knee. None of us has met John yet.

We all draw a deep breath at nine-thirty and find our coats.

'Thank you for coming,' said Cathy one night when our group met at her place. The way she said it, you knew she felt the whole house had received a blessing through the group meeting there. I never quite saw it that way before.

Thursday is our day off. We try and put the pressures out of our minds for the day, but often of course, Christopher and I talk about how we really feel and in comes the parish to the conversation. We talk it through and then find it easier to forget.

Regretfully, we say No when someone asks for the key of the church. You would think it was simple enough, wouldn't you? Just give them the key and let them enjoy the building. Nine times out of ten this is what happens, but there always seemed to be some complication on Thursdays and we would end up spending half an hour seeing to someone and feeling it was work that we should never have let ourselves in for.

The crunch came when two tutors asked if their students could sketch inside the church on a particular Wednesday and Thursday. Nothing simpler—show them the ropes on Wednesday and they can look after themselves on Thursday.

At lunch-time the church bell rang. There is no mistaking it for any other sound. I went over, wondering if the church key was playing up and the students couldn't get out.

The first thing I heard was the organ being played—badly. Arrived in the gallery, I couldn't take it in at first; a student was smoking while he played our precious, inflammable instrument. He was also wearing his hat but that was secondary.

'I'm sorry,' I said, 'but people can't play the organ without special permission, as it's so old. And there's a heavy fire risk too. Could you put your fag out?' He was abusive, so I thought I had better go and get Christopher, day off or not.

But first I asked them all why they had rung the bell; they denied it and were indignant that I had gone in to 'check up' on them.

'But I only came because I heard the bell ring,' I said. 'We thought you were locked in or something.' The tutors had gone off, leaving the students working. We turfed everyone out of church and asked them to explain why to their tutors.

Since then, we have said that the church is not available to anyone on Thursdays; then we can welcome them on the other days.

We both enjoy a quiet day, reading, pottering around the house or garden, free not to have to go out. But sometimes on a bright autumn day, we put a Mars bar in our pockets and go out for a walk.

Where does one go for a walk in the inner city? We have four places; the first is cheating because we catch a bus to get there. The Embankment of the river Thames affords views and interest all the way from the Tower of London to Vauxhall Bridge. (Hazards too, with all the new building going on.)

Often in a narrow street, there is no room to step back and enjoy the different roof levels and styles of architecture, but looking across the river you have the space to see the whole picture in perspective. It is backed by the rising modern skyline and fronted by the trees and the river.

Walking ankle-deep in autumn leaves, I felt I was seeing St Thomas's Hospital for the first time. The Festival Hall looks quite different when you are not in charge of twenty excited children going to a concert there. Both sides of the river, but not on the same afternoon, I recommend the Embankment.

A shorter walk is down the Isle of Dogs, with all the new building that makes it look like something out of a space-age film set. We met Julia walking home one day.

'I come down here for a walk every week,' she said, 'simply to have a look. It's different every time.' We take our friends down there to see it; no-one would have dreamed of doing that five years ago. The sunlight gleams on the water and the new Docklands Light Railway soars gracefully across the docks and the wharves, twenty feet above them all.

Different again is our third walk—Regent's Canal, northward from Limehouse. Miles of towpath and seclusion. A few anglers, a few dogs taking their owners for a walk, one or two cyclists. The sad thing is, the canal is almost empty of boats. Just the occasional long-boat on hire to a school, a few barges in Camden Lock, and the Canoe Club splashing and shouting, clad in orange life-jackets, just above Mile End.

The good thing is, the towpath has been refurbished, with brick paving beside each lock and plenty of access points; it has become a local amenity instead of a forgotten asset. There is nowhere quite like it on a winter's afternoon, walking north-west with the bridges etched against a flaming sky and the flotsam crunching against the icefloes beside our feet.

Every bridge is a different shape and each stretch of canal, between two bridges, has a character of its own—derelict warehouses, smart new dwellings or a rural quarter of a mile, complete with a seat. The boundary of the towpath might be railings beside a street or brick walls, mellow in the sunshine. Walking up the canal with the boys used to be a hair-raising experience. Any mother will guess that they fished things out of the canal, teetering on the edge and chucking water at each other. No family of boys would settle for less.

What you might not expect is that Jonathan and

Timothy see every bridge as a challenge. They stand one on either side and throw a tennis ball up and over. What a bus driver would do, roaring down Kingsland Road, if he encountered the Idles' ball soaring across from parapet to parapet in front of his windscreen, I cannot imagine.

There is one more place for walking—a square mile of peace tucked away between the branching railway lines and the old streets of Bow. It is called Mile End Cemetery.

Forget wide hillsides covered with white graves, lying open to the sky. Think of a mature wood where birds and small wild animals can live undisturbed. Among the trees are old graves, row upon row of small graves of the nineteen thirties, covered with ivy. Row upon row of medium sized graves with hugh trees growing out of them. Avenues of once splendid Victorian graves, with gravel paths between them leading from sunlight into shade and out again. Outcrops of enormous family vaults and a stunning Gothic folly.

Christopher, Jonathan, Jeremy and I sauntered along under the trees one afternoon, crunching the dead leaves. I had taken the twins walking in there once but had not gone too deep into the wood. Today, with my menfolk, I was completely safe.

We worked our way eastwards, towards the sunlight and the diverging network of railway lines. 'That's where I got lost the other night,' said Christopher, pointing to the waste ground beyond the wall. 'Lived here for twelve years and never been that way before.'

We wandered back into the thick wood and passed a brick plinth with a memorial stone set into it.

> This garden commemorates the lives
> of 190 people of Poplar
> who were among those killed
> in air raids within the borough
> 1939–1945
> and whose mortal remains rest in this place.

The garden has been taken over by the trees and the undergrowth; the air of deep tranquillity remains.

We came out into a clearing where the grass slopes down to the railings beside Cantrell Road. Jonathan never goes for a walk without a football and here was the ideal pitch. I sat down and watched them, keeping half an eye on the road behind me.

All over East London there are railway arches. And everywhere, there are small car repair firms housed in the arches. Here at the southern boundary of the cemetery, the cars spill out into Cantrell Road so that even cycling along it is hazardous. There are smart cars under repair, crumpled cars that will never go again, piles of junk, piles of tyres, piles of cars.

There were lights on under some of the arches and cheerful sounds echoing out into the road—whistling, banging and Radio 1.

'Well, tell you what, give me a couple of hours and I'll see what I can do with it,' said someone, leaning on a car, unhurried. He was wearing oily jeans, an oily sweatshirt and a brown cap—a young West Indian with an East London voice.

I kicked the football back into play and jumped around a bit; the sun was below the chimney line and the afternoon became chilly. Another ten minutes and we began to think of a wood fire and tea. As we walked towards the gate a car reversed down the road at speed, zigzagging between the battered cars and piles of scrap. Christopher laughed.

'I bet that's not his own car,' he said.

We went along beside the arches for a bit; tyres and then stored timber, lorries and then a stone mason's. There was a gravestone in Hebrew and, tilted against the opposite doorway, one in Bengali. Then an angel above 'George Morrison'. We turned sharp left under the railway and were back in the noise of the traffic.

Friday is catching up day, baking day—and this week Anne and Grace are bringing their children to draw the church windows. We love having classes in church; they are always full of questions and on their best behaviour.

We sit them in the front pews to start with, explain that this is a Christian church and say a short prayer. Then we talk about the project they have come for and say, 'Any questions?' Plenty, ranging from 'How many windows are there?' to 'Why did Jesus die?' The answers have to be brief.

Then they are off, wandering around the church, or lying flat on their stomachs to draw laboriously or asking to be taken up into the gallery. Christopher takes them up the stairs and shows them around; I come across Hong Ha filling a page with beautifully drawn windows.

'There are some different shapes in the porch,' I say. 'Shall I show you?'

Forty minutes later they all depart, waving and saying Thank you. Next week their drawings will be up on the classroom wall and I will be able to admire them.

Anything can happen on a Saturday. The social life of the church from a seaside outing to a spring-cleaning of the vestries; or a march to save the Mildmay Hospital. We did, or at least we helped!

The best Saturdays are those on which nothing happens and I am free to get ready for Sunday calmly and then do some gardening.

'You're nearer God's 'eart in a garden, lady,' said the caretaker from next door. And there's bound to be someone going past when I am in the front garden, calling out, 'Yoohoo . . . You're busy!' Yes, but I'm enjoying it. Weeding and pruning may well do the garden good but they do me even more good. Tugging up dandelions helps to bring peace and order to my mind.

November is wonderful; no more weeds running riot until next spring; once the leaves are all raked up, the garden will be reasonably tidy for weeks. Granted, they take some raking. Standing there on our tiny patch of lawn, ankle deep in red and gold leaves, you would think we had ten cherry trees.

I might, in November, make a foray into the West End. The flocks of tourists have flown home, leaving only a few hardy members of the species. The lights are not yet switched on in Oxford Street. I could dash into a bookshop and buy some presents. And there are a few odd jobs I have been saving up for this kind of a day.

A One-day Travel Card, currently at £2.00, takes you on any bus or tube; you can bus-hop as much as you need to. We might grumble about the buses and their infrequent appearance, but the Travel Card is a bargain.

Hold on for dear life when the one-man bus brakes sharply.

'Like I said,' I heard someone behind me say, as we shot forward in our seats, 'if you ain't got a slipped disc when you get on the bus, you'll 'ave one before you get off.'

I remember one of these rare visits to town. I began by going up to the top of Gloucester Place to take some old spectacles to the Baptist Missionary Society. Then, a raid on the biggest Marks & Spencer's in town, a succulent peach off a barrow for lunch and a look into the bookshops. My last stop was a venerable establishment where I could buy Christopher some clerical collars.

I went in quietly, looked around and tried the left-hand showroom. My small footsteps were drowned by the heavy tread of a servant of the establishment, entering the room with me. I discovered later that his name was Frank. Frank and I found ourselves looking at the rear end of a second servant of the establishment, who was casting about in a cupboard under the window.

'Er . . . Bill . . . ,' said Frank. 'The Bishop of Sherborne is here. He'd like a new cassock.'

'I don't care if he wants knickers to match,' said Bill. 'You look after him.'

Frank's face twitched. The old firm was tottering on the brink of disgrace.

'Er . . . Bill . . . ,' he said. 'There's a lady here.'

'Well, look after her too, will you?' said Bill.

I felt so sorry for Frank, as I followed him to the collar department, that I paused to admire a cassock-alb.

'Lovely embroidery,' I said.

But he was not to be cheered. In gloom he sold me the collars, while a junior waited upon the Bishop of Sherborne, and in gloom he escorted me to the door.

But I laughed all the way to the bus-stop.

10

Once in Royal David's City

O come let us adore him,
Christ the LORD!

The warmth of the school building wrapped around me like a hug after the raw December cold outside. I pushed open the door of the hall and walked into the murmur of two hundred voices, the warmth of two hundred bodies and a general air of bustle and good humour.

The Christmas Fayre at Stepney Greencoat School was in full swing. Teachers and older children manned the stalls, Peter Green the Head sauntered through the crowd having a friendly word with everyone and toddlers pulled their mothers towards the ice-cream counter.

I made a beeline for the cakes; anyone who has tasted Peggy's cooking wants more. She put a chocolate sponge under her stall for me to collect later. Next, the second-hand books but Peter waylaid me.

'I've got a message for you,' he said. 'Wendy says will you write something for her for Easter.' Will I write something for . . . It would have been dignified to say, 'Please tell her I shall be delighted' but what I actually said was, 'Yeah, fine.'

I drifted over to the auction of large household goods where Peter was starting to shout his wares. With a voice that would stop any town planner in his tracks, he was known affectionately as a one-man Rent-a-mob by the local Road Action Group.

'Here's a nice two-wheeler bike for a seven year old. What am I bid?' roared Peter. Christopher joined me and bid for a mirror with Snoopy on, for Marcus. I remember buying some new plimsolls on the jumble stall and combing the bookstall for paperbacks.

But all that I could think of was that Wendy had asked me to write something. I was not under the illusion that I was Mrs Christian Writer of the Year. She just wanted something printable, tidy and on time. It seems a long while ago now but that was how I got started, writing for a Parish Magazine inset.

In December we visit every door in the parish with an invitation to the Carol Service. People sometimes say, 'Nobody from the church has ever visited me.'

When the population moves along so quickly that could well be true but at least once a year, we go.

That year, three nights each week a small group met in the rectory to pray and collect invitation cards. One night I went with Colleen and Mike to brand new flats in Rhodeswell Road; some of them were still getting sorted out. Another night Colleen and I went to Piggott Street—a postman's nightmare.

'We might as well go right along this landing while we're here,' I said. But Colleen was adamant.

'That would get us in a muddle,' she said. 'That part of the landing is called Kildare Walk; we ought to stick to Piggott Street and do the numbers consecutively.' So we stuck. By the end of the evening we were sure the planners of the estate were barmy—but we had visited every house in Piggott Street.

People at this end of the parish were friendly, pleased to see us, thought the idea of Carols by Candlelight was very nice, but on the whole preferred watching television to going to church and would rather get back to it now than talk about God.

'Oh Jerusalem, Jerusalem, if only you knew. . . .'

And Limehouse too.

Another night, Ruth and I went down the road, past my school to the estate where most of the children live whom I teach on Wednesdays. This was a very different way of visiting.

'Hallo Mrs Idle. . . . Where are you going Miss?. . . . Can I come with you?. . . . Mum, it's Mrs Idle, she's in our school. . . .' So in all the English-speaking homes there are friendly conversations and at opposite ends of each landing or side by side, Ruth and I could say, 'Why don't you bring your Mum to the Carol Service? You ought to see it, all in candle-light. Lovely!'

In the hard-to-let flats you find students. A few said coldly, 'No thanks, I don't believe in God.' One looked at me in speechless amazement and his friend, behind him, called out, 'I say Lionel, guess what? Bernard has just been invited to church!' They accepted a card; I wonder what they did with it. You just have to go on to the next door, praying as you go that the bright candle and the words 'O come let us adore him' will be the first small stepping stone towards their one day seeking for this Lord, whom Christians adore.

One block of flats in particular seems hostile year after year.

'Wait till you get to the door next to the staircase,' I said to Ruth. 'They're practising Roman Catholics.' I came and leaned over her shoulder as the door opened; two smiling children and a mother with a gentle face. We had not called to coax them away from their own church, but merely to wish them a happy Christmas and to enlist their prayers as we went along. After the rebuffs on the landings above, it did us good to stand there for a moment, feeling the love from that home.

Sadly, pensioners would say, 'Oh, is it from the church? I'll get my purse.'

It gave us the opportunity to say it was a free invitation, like God's love, but a lot of them would not feel safe going out to the Carol Service after dark.

And that leaves less than half the estate accounted for. Many of my small friends from school are members of the other half and without their help it would be difficult to visit. You knock on the door and an Asian mother opens it—maybe Chinese or Vietnamese, more likely Bengali.

'Good evening,' you say. 'This is an invitation for you. We are singing carols by candlelight in St Anne's church.' You pause and smile and the mother smiles back shyly. Then she turns and calls. Out pops Lim or Kwok or Hamida, grins and says inevitably, 'Hallo Miss.'

Now is the time to choose your words carefully because they are going to be translated by a child who may not know the words for church or carols. I usually begin by saying,

'I expect you are Muslims, are you?' very gently, so we all know where we are. Then I explain that we are going to sing songs about Jesus, like the ones we sing in school, and everyone is invited. It will be in the big church in the churchyard, the one they pass when they go to the library.

"Please tell Mummy,' I say, 'that we are her friends.' The child translates and the mother smiles shyly again.

'Tell her that Jesus is our Lord'—I bow my head and put my hands together—'and we keep his birthday at Christmas. And we wish you all a happy Christmas.'

More smiles and I move on to the next house. Here there is a row of shoes in the hall and the father of the family comes to the door in a loose-fitting white suit.

'Oh, you are Muslims,' I say with a smile, and tell him about Jesus Christ being our Lord.

'Don't forget we are your friends,' and I leave him with a card to remind him.

Ruth catches me up and we go down the stairs to the next landing, where we seem to be in danger of being eaten alive by the hound of the Baskervilles. We stand together until Rover has been shut in the kitchen. Christopher had an entire pocket ripped off his duffle coat on one visit—to people he knew, but I have not been bitten since I was a district nurse.

Then we split up once more, to each end of the landing. At one house, the Bengali mother was very shy and reluctant to accept a card. But the door of the house I had just been visiting flew open again and there was a crossfire of conversation, punctuated with smiles towards me. Apparently Nassim had told his mother I was a friend and she was relaying this to her neighbour. So I was able to leave a card, a reminder of Christ at Christmas, after all.

On the Saturday evening before the Carol Service I was dead beat but I wasn't telling Christopher. I had promised to visit Donne House with invitations and to Donne House I would go if I had to crawl there.

All too often, it seems to me, especially if I am feeling depressed or overworked, people say they are ever so sorry but they can't come after all. But they expect the Rector to do his work and theirs as well. So I wasn't joining that gang.

As we sat there, ready to pray and go, I said, 'Lord, what am I going to do? My legs are like jelly. Please help me Lord. How are you going to help me?'

We prayed and picked up our piles of cards, and I lingered by the door, hoping for I knew not what. I was going alone tonight. Christopher was pointing out a block of flats on the parish map, to one of the others.

'No need for you to wait, dear,' he said kindly. When I reached the front door, Colin caught me up.

'I know it sounds silly when we're only going round the corner,' he said. 'I was going to walk along with you—but—would you like a lift?' The first half of the miracle had happened. Now I only had five floors to walk up. Or had I? At the end of Dodd Street I hopped out of the car and walked across the courtyard. There was a pensioner with a couple of friends, standing by the lift.

'Goodnight Ethel.'

'See you tomorrow then. Goodnight Fred.'

'Thanks Sid. Goodnight.'

He pressed the lift-call button and stood there, an East Ender who wouldn't hurt a fly.

'Are you going up? Can I come with you? I'm scared of lifts,' I said. He looked at me in some surprise.

'How far up do you want to go then? All right—if you think it's all right for you to come up in the lift with me.' I beamed at him.

'Yes, I think it's quite all right. Thank you,' I said. He lived on the fourth floor but he took me to the fifth and I gave him an invitation before he sailed down to the fourth again.

The miracle was complete. I could manage the rest.

People ask me quite often about the streets of Limehouse at night and how safe I feel. Do I go out?

I never take a handbag or money; just a jingle of busfare in a pocket if I need it and a plastic shopping bag if there is something to carry—like a Bible. You can run faster with a bag on your wrist than with a book in your hand and it is easier, bookless, to grab an assailant's ankle. I always read articles about self-defence when I come across them and the one thing I have absorbed is—Scream, and if you can't run, grab your man by the ankle.

The local paper is full of ghastly stories; you would think somebody got mugged in every street every week. They don't. But none of us would dare to say 'It could never happen to me.'

When we go visiting round the parish we always aim to finish at nine o'clock; we don't expect anyone to answer the door after that. We try to visit the elderly, where we know them, well before then.

Time and again we say to some little old lady, 'Haven't you got a chain on your door? Shouldn't you see who it is before you open it?' And they sheepishly agree that they are not being careful enough.

The important part is prevention; I wouldn't walk

down an isolated footpath or go past an empty warehouse. If you find God calling you to an area like ours, you work out what you need to do and where you want to go at night, and then get on with it, alert and careful.

I was walking through the flats to our group Bible study one winter's night when I heard soft padding footsteps approaching. I marched on, ready to shout, sock him one and run. The padding came closer and slowed down.

'Hi Marjorie, had a good weekend?' said David, also on his way to our group.

December is an erratic month, with days in a row when you are more than busy doing extra jobs for Christmas and then a couple of quiet days when there might even be time to put a duster round the bedrooms. I have known a bedroom to survive the whole month without being dusted. It is much more important to write a longer letter to a friend, do a bit more recorder practice or simply put your feet up. December ought to be a warm and happy month with time to care about people, not a frantic bad-tempered month with no time to stop.

I seized a quiet afternoon in the first week to get six dozen mince pies into the freezer and work out a sequence of carols for recorders. Both these jobs were for the Carol Service, which attracts the biggest congregation of the year.

Jonathan, Ruth Day and I had to plan fifteen minutes of music to play before the service. We found, the first year we did it, that key changes could be a major disaster, so each year we begin in the key of F, working our way forward through 'Carols for Choirs' and the 'Anglican Hymn Book'. Then we flip the pages back and play some carols in G, rising to the heights of a couple in D at the end.

So it all has to be worked out carefully, some from last year and some new ones. I asked Lyn to finish her voluntaries with something in F and we would begin gently on her last chord with 'Away in a manger'. The acoustics in our church are superb and, amateurs though we are, we try to exploit it.

Halfway through December I had enough bread, butter and sausages in the freezer and enough tea, sugar and baked beans in the pantry to see us through until January. The freezer is a gift from friends who went to Malawi and needed a good home for it; it becomes a good friend at festival times. The cake was in Jeremy's bedroom out of the way, covered in marzipan and awaiting a quiet evening for icing. The chicken was ordered and there were a couple of shepherd's pies for our next two Sunday dinners. Now I could forget food for a few days and concentrate on school.

There were two special engagements at each school. Stepney Greencoat put on an Entertainment for all the parents and friends one week and came to church for their Carol Service the next. Cyril Jackson school put on an evening pantomine for the parents one week and had an End of Term Assembly the next. For the pantomime this time, my only duty was to play 'After the ball was over' at the end.

For the Assembly I needed to be subtle. The Head's idea of 'Just a couple of carols that everyone knows' needed a little work if it was to be successful. So I said to him in passing, 'Is it OK by you if the top floor juniors drop in this morning to practise a couple of carols?' It was. A consultation with the four teachers and I had all the top juniors settling down on the hall floor for twenty minutes' carol practice. We included a new one —

> 'Come and sing the Christmas story
> this holy night'

which goes to 'All through the night' just as one of the new harvest hymns does.

Then it was back to recorders for church.

'I'm not too fond of "The holly and the ivy" said Jonathan. 'Could we cut it out?'

Church organists may have to play hymns that irritate them but it would be crazy for us to play something that did not suit us. So we abandoned 'The holly'; maybe next time he would feel differently about it.

Our last practice was on Sunday morning after church, while everyone was still drinking coffee. Then home for a quick lunch with Colin, Paul and Ruth as guests. We were going to have a working afternoon.

Until now, setting up the candles for the Carol Service had been a family affair, a long cold afternoon's work. There had been so many things to pioneer when we first came; now it was time to hand this job over to others.

Today there were nine of us, all knowing what we were doing, and it took an hour. Nine man-hours. We laid trestle-tables over the far ends of the pews and covered them with crepe paper. On these we stood all the small candlesticks the church possesses. The larger ones were clustered at the front to give light to readers and preacher.

While two people were taping long poles—each carrying three candles—to the ends of the pews, five or six others were sorting and whittling candles to fit into the great variety of candlesticks.

Marcus, nimble-fingered, slipped a duplicated Order of Service into each Bethlehem Carol sheet. Jeremy and Timothy set up the lights on the Christmas tree. When we had finished, there was a forest of candles.

We always think for one frightening moment—suppose nobody comes? The rain poured down that evening and we knew it would keep the pensioners at John Lawder House indoors.

We were wrong. Helped along by Fred and some of our younger members, they arrived triumphantly together with a hundred or so others, and settled themselves down for a feast of carols and Bible readings.

Our neighbours across the road were having a move-around supper, with each course in a different house. It was Bob and Margo's idea, with the Carol Service as the first course. So Jerry of the Rolls Royce and Peter of the Revolution found themselves in church too.

Not that Ruth, Jon and I saw any of them as we sat under the three small electric lights in the archway at the side of the chancel. We played carefully, gaining more confidence with each carol safely done. At six-twenty-nine we played 'The first Nowell' and relaxed.

Switch off the lights, move into the south aisle, stand still for the notices and slide into our seats when everyone stands for the first carol.

There is something comfortable and reassuring about a carol service; a family gathering with lots of hymns we all know. So we have one or two new ones each time, to make us sit up and say, 'Hey, what's this?' and listen more carefully.

They were singing the last hymn —

Adam's likeness Lord, efface
Stamp thine image in its place.
O, to all Thyself impart
Formed in each believing heart.
Hark, the herald angels sing
Glory to the new-born king.

Reluctantly I slipped out of church. The rain had stopped, the sky was bright with stars and I was desperately tired. But it would be another two hours before I could stop. I must be careful, steel myself against the spilt tea, the crumbs ground into the carpet, the tired small children larking around. The crypt room had not yet been built.

I ran into the warm house, switched on all the lights, made the tea and unloaded the mince pies from the oven—not only mine but gifts of six or ten at a time from various church members. The first guest rang the bell.

'Welcome,' I said. We served about sixty cups of tea and ten beakers of orange; plenty of willing hands helped with the trays and plenty more did the washing up. And when everyone had gone home I was left with an embarrassment—more mince pies than I had started with!

The one important job I had to do on Christmas Eve was to visit George, a church member who was in hospital. We knew he had been shopping in November and wrapped a lot of presents, and they had followed him around when he moved hospitals; he would want his friends to have them. Where were they?

Christopher had paved the way and now it was my job to get hold of them. I wondered how George would look; only a fortnight ago Christopher and I, on different visits, had stood beside his bed, over at Denmark Hill, gazing down at the bandages, the tubes and his unconscious person. We had held his unresponding hand and said a prayer.

And here he was, walking down the corridor towards me smiling.

'Do you remember buying Christmas presents for us all—Lily and David and everybody?' I asked. George shook his head. He remembered the names, they were his friends. But the presents were a mystery. So a nurse came with us to check his locker and there they all were, generously chosen and carefully wrapped, just waiting for Father Christmas.

We checked the parcels one by one.

' "Barbara"—is that David's wife or Wendy's Mum?' I asked. 'And who is Joyce?'

'Oh, she's the physiotherapist,' said staff nurse.

By the time they were all sorted and piled up, I could have done with a sleigh and a reindeer or two.

We wandered back into the corridor; the television was on full blast in the day-room so we stayed outside, talking about our friends at church. There seemed to be large gaps in George's memory. Soon he was tired; it was time to go.

We must have looked a funny pair—I was all bundled up in woollies and wellies against the Arctic cold of Mile End and he was wearing a droopy hospital dressing gown. We clasped hands and bowed our heads, frail human beings in direct communication with heaven.

'Lighten our darkness . . .' we said. There was a lot of darkness still to come for George, but his eyes always light up when we share the name of Jesus together.

The parcels grew heavy as I walked down Eric Street; I changed hands at the zebra crossing and caught sight of the twins waving frantically. I looked down at their small faces, rosy with frost, bright with joy.

'I've got new boots. Watch me jump,' said Alex and Michael said breathlessly, 'Auntie Marjorie, did you know it's Christmas tomorrow?'

Christopher had been busy on visits too. We met in the kitchen, put the kettle on and switched on the radio.

'Once in Royal David's city . . .' sang the choirboy in King's College Chapel. Christmas had begun.

About eleven o'clock, after a rest, a bath and fried eggs all round, I gathered up a few small gifts and the music I needed and wrapped myself up warmly. The gifts were mostly Thank you tokens—a tin of flapjack or a home-made candle.

The church tower was white against the night sky and I stood there for a moment, all by myself, enjoying the quiet moment. Tonight the pain and the battles of the past year were forgotten; the Christian family was coming to church to say Thank you to God for his priceless gift.

We had candle-light again. It was dark up in the gallery as I switched on the organ-motor and swung the angle-poise lamp over the console. Below me, the forest of candles and a smaller forest of heads.

There was a crowd of strangers, I discovered, when I went down for Communion. When I was younger I used to feel they had no right to drop in just for one service in the year; nowadays I know that their faith and mine needs to be strengthened, and here in church, strength can be found.

The strangers were quickly away afterwards but the church family were relaxed and full of conversation. I had a candle for each of my fellow Explorer leaders.

'You can't eat it. Not expensive but very fragile,' I said lightly, but my thoughts were elsewhere. After the manger, the cross. Oxford . . . a misty October morning in 1555. Hugh Latimer and Nicholas Ridley were being burnt at the stake for their adherence to the truth of the Bible. 'Be of good comfort, Master Ridley, and play the man; we shall this day light such a candle, by God's grace in England, as I trust never shall be put out.'

Nor has it. They no longer burn people at the stake. They found other ways of dealing with Alexander Solzhenitsyn and Archbishop Janani Luwum and Martin Luther King.

> Grant O Lord, that, in all our sufferings
> here upon earth for the testimony of thy
> truth, we may steadfastly look up to
> heaven, and by faith behold the glory
> that shall be revealed . . .

On Christmas Day I always wake with a stab of fear. Will it happen again? One year Christopher was very quiet over breakfast, while we opened just a few family presents.

When we had all finished he said, 'I went over to put the heat on and found the church had been burgled. Could the older ones come and help me clear up the mess?' The boys seem to cope with these things much better than we do; the three eldest went over with Christopher while Marcus and I tackled the washing up and got the dinner under way.

The burglars must have been slightly drunk or they

would never have attempted anything so crazy. Having broken a window in the west porch and found they could not get through into the church, they piled chairs and tables dangerously, recklessly and climbed up to the windows at the back of the organ. They broke one, got through and went on down into the body of the church.

Arrived here, they found there was nothing much they could do. They took the orange squash and coffee out of the cupboard and then set to work on all the Christmas cards on the table at the back of the church.

The cards were addressed to church members—an internal postal system—and none contained, as far as we knew, anything valuable. The burglars opened every one, leaving them strewn over the floor.

The incredible part was, they had to leave the same way as they had come—out through the broken organ window, down the pile of chairs and tables and then out through the porch window. They left a trail of broken glass leading down from the organ.

By ten, Christopher and the boys had put the church to rights. Perhaps at last, we could dare to relax.

Yes, Lord, we greet thee
Born this happy morning. . . .

11

Cold in the city

O ye Dews and Frosts, bless ye the Lord;
praise him, and magnify him for ever.
O ye Frost and Cold, bless ye the Lord;
praise him, and magnify him for ever.
(Benedicite).

I stand in our small walled garden, quite still. It is a January afternoon; the earth stands hard as iron, the leaves on the primulas motionless and frozen. The whole garden is still. The wind fell yesterday and everything is waiting for the snow.

The branches of the forsythia bush are etched against the leaden grey sky; on the mellow brick wall the winter jasmine is bright with yellow blossom.

Suddenly a pile of dry leaves rustles in the still air and the blackbird, bright-eyed, lifts hurriedly, his mouth full of insects. He sits on the wall and finishes his lunch. Then he scolds me for invading his garden. He and his forbears have been scolding me for the past ten years; they think they own this small patio bordered by flowerbeds. They are a brave, vociferous family—sometimes almost reckless. We found one of them terrorising the neighbour's cat one day; and with a jealous black fury keeping an eye on the garden it is very rare for a pigeon to try a visit.

'Can't I eat my dinner in peace, you interfering old woman?' the blackbird shouted.

'Listen mate,' I told him. 'I came out here to batten down the hatches. It's going to snow. Look at all the mess you've made, pulling out leaves on to the patio and spiking up the moss between the paving. I've got to sweep it all up before the snow spreads it around. There's the bonfire remains to clear away and the washing to take in.'

I begin and he watches me—or should I say, supervises me? Then he makes for home, somewhere over in the churchyard, and I stand there for a moment longer, with a pile of damp shirts over my arm. What will January bring? Will we have a lot of snow this year?

The first flakes eddy down and I go in. Time to stock up with tins and bread; it is the time when some of my regular callers spend more on fuel than usual and then come to ask for food. Who can blame them? I always have a few tins of beef stew and vegetables—'Ready meal' it says on the label—and some spare bread. Occasionally they ask for cheese or eggs but I resist this; I'm glad to help but this isn't a grocer's shop.

'Fill up with bread and potatoes now,' I say, 'and then buy your own cheese when you get your next lot of money.'

The snow begins to swirl outside the kitchen window. Perhaps this year we'd better have the Explorers' party in the house instead of the crypt. Cosier. I always enjoy doing a big bake, the other leaders chip in with their own specialities and someone wraps pencils and sweets for Pass the Parcel. Are we dotty to have the annual party in January, when life is at its most difficult? We are wondering whether to change it to November when ice and snow and coughs and colds are less plentiful.

Whatever the time of year, it is exhausting running a party for children. But enjoyable. I just wish that boys of nine wouldn't fight when the others are Spinning the Plate.

Sometimes we have combined Explorers and Climbers (aged three to seven) and had one big party. Plenty of

Lego and small toys at the sides of the room for those who don't want to join in the games, plenty of helpers with comfy laps and plenty of time for actually eating, means that the whole range of children can enjoy the party.

Looking back, every party seems much like every other party; I hope that means they were well-run and happy. Every year there are children who have never played the Farmer's in his Den or Ring on String; their new-found enjoyment adds to the fun. And every year there are the veterans who forget the quickest way to Catch the Train and put the gloves on first.

There was a lot of snow one year, trains were cancelled and stations deep in the countryside were cut off. So Ruth brought Indeg with her to help at the party.

'I've never heard that name before,' said Marcus. 'Where does she come from?' and he looked round the kitchen door expecting to see an Asian.

'Well, I'm a friend of Ruth's, so where do you think?' she said with the same lovely lilt in her voice as Ruth's. 'Wales is deep in snow and I can't get home, so here I am.' And welcome she was.

More pairs of willing hands are always needed to help pass the sandwiches and replace burst balloons. Not to mention helping everyone into their wellingtons and making sure they all had a balloon and a gingerbread man when they went out into the slippery evening.

The cold weather always brings extra callers, a hundred different hard-up stories waiting to be told on the door-step.

'Please help me to cope with this one, Lord, whoever it might be,' I ask when the doorbell rings. To find Rhona there or Hilda, dropping by to confer about church coffee or flowers is always a relief. Or perhaps just the man to read the meters. One of them asked me about the block of renovated flats next door.

'The world is such a funny place these days,' he said, taking the cellar stairs carefully. 'Are you the reverend's wife? Ah. . . .' There are obviously matters that can be mentioned to a reverend's wife that cannot be mentioned to a mere other wife. Or even, says Christopher, to a mere reverend.

'They're all living in sin these days. Strordenry. Strordenry. All the women are Ms you know instead of Mrs. All these flats being turned into posh places. East London isn't what it was. I don't take it upon myself to judge. I merely mention that it's quite Hickstrordenry.'

But most of our cold weather callers have no jobs and no pronouncements to make upon the lives of their fellow men and women. The unfortunate, the gullible and the alcohol dependent, all wanting the fare to Birmingham or Glasgow, or a bed for the night, or a cup of tea and a sandwich. The fare to Birmingham just buys a bottle of whisky nicely.

We never give money. Christopher is able to give a note, to be taken to the Salvation Army Hostel, to say he will pay the cost of a bed for the night. This comes out of a special fund. Both of us give cups of tea and sandwiches. Often a man will be adamant that he must have money or he must see the vicar, and no other person in the world has suffered as much misfortune as he, but when I offer him a cup of tea instead, he will soften and be grateful. Here is someone who is actually bothering to do something for him, has actually offered to give him something.

'God bless you, lady,' he says.

I never invite anyone in, however bad the weather. Alone in the house or with Christopher in the study, it would be foolish. They could be troublesome, refuse to go—anything. So it makes it fair for everyone if they stay outside, and it gives me the freedom to be friendly at a safe distance.

Twice we have had teenagers whom we knew, knocking at the door. They had run away from home and somehow thought we could wave a magic wand and put everything right. Christopher walked home with one of them because she said her father would beat her up for staying out.

'Are you all right?' I asked anxiously when he returned.

He laughed.

"There was this mild little bloke sitting at the kitchen table in his shirt sleeves, reading—of all things—*The Times*. He didn't turn a hair.' I guess that was the real problem.

Alcoholic women are harder to deal with than men; I never know where I am with them. They can tell the most heart-rending tales about their starving little children at home; not a word of it is true. One of them came barefoot and asked for shoes. I rummaged in the cellar and had to come up when the doorbell rang again. There was no-one else on the step.

'What is it?' I asked the barefoot woman.

'I thought you were taking too long,' she said. There are times when I long to stand on the roof and have a good scream.

'Don't be so silly,' I told her. 'I'm not a magician. I'm looking as fast as I can. If you ring the bell again I shan't answer.' All I could find in her size were plimsolls but she was grateful.

It was another alcoholic woman who pushed her luck rather far. I had only noticed her that morning for the first time, wandering along Salmon Lane with a dog. I came home with the shopping, put the kettle on and saw this girl coming up the path. She would be asking for food. But instead of the doorbell ringing, there was a chink of milk bottles on the other step and there she was going down the path with a pint of milk in her hand. From the gate onwards she ran, surprisingly fast for a barefoot—yes another—barefoot alcoholic. I caught her up under the railway bridge and politely asked for my milk back.

'I haven't got any milk,' she said. By this time it was in her plastic shopping bag. I looked in and took out mine. What I was sorely tempted to do was to take out the other pint and deliver it back to Margo's doorstep across the road. But instinct was held in check by reason—how could I prove any such thing?—and I left it there, only to discover later that Margo had indeed lost a pint that morning.

'You're a thief, a blank, blank thief,' shouted the woman after me, to the huge enjoyment of two passing neighbours. I turned back.

'Well, you know where I live,' I said. Poor soul, I hope she enjoyed Margo's milk.

We came home late one night from a school Parents' Evening and Marcus, aged about twelve at the time, ran on ahead. He strolled back to us looking thoughtful.

'There's someone lying on the grass in our garden,' he said, 'and I think he's dead.'

We went into the house and found a torch. Christopher approached the recumbent body and prodded it. It sat up. It was Ken, still full of drink, chatty and affable. He bade us all goodnight—'Au revoir, Messieurs et Madame'—and went home. He is a Geordie seaman, no longer working, as strong as an ox in spite of all the alcohol.

One cold night he called, angry and ready to murder someone—I didn't understand who—because they had been shouting at him. I shivered a little as I stood there; but let him talk and he would soon forget his grievance and start talking about Robbie Burns, and then go home happy. He leaned against the front door, holding the big brass knob to balance it and himself. He screwed up his face and narrowed his eyes.

'Rich and poor. What a contrast! Sometimes I think I'd rather live in Russia.'

'Oh, I expect there are plenty of starving peasants over there,' I said to provoke him.

'Did I ever tell you what Robbie Burns said?' he asked.

Yes, more than once.

'What was that, Ken?'

'Robbie Burns said, "The more I see of human nature, the more I love my dog." And by the way, I'm worried about yon collie. The one that lives on the corner. He's pining for his master. I know collies, we breed them on the Border. He's pining. . . . Ah well, I must be going.' He straightened up and his face cleared. He looked at me wistfully and I held out my hand. He kissed it fervently and then said with a sudden twinkle, 'Don't wash yer hand for a week!'

'Goodnight, Ken. God bless you.'

'Shalom,' he roared and went down the steps. I held my hand under the tap, sad at all the alcoholic waste of strength and sweetness, gifts and guts that goes on all around us.

Ken was obviously missing Dame Edith Ramsey. For decades she had worked for the poor and the poorest, Jew and Gentile, in East London. Every Sunday night at Christ Church Spitalfields, after the Evening Service, Ken used to kiss her goodnight and she, great lady that she was, never flinched. Now she was in heaven and Ken felt the need to find someone else who would listen to him extolling Robert Burns.

I went back into the kitchen and switched on the iron again. Next door, in the dining-room the Parochial Church Council was ironing out the problems of the local church. I never knew, until we came to a parish, how tricky a PCC meeting can be. Twelve people all wanting to do the will of God and all seeing the agenda slightly differently. They had not laughed for ages. Was it a very fraught meeting?

Suddenly I heard Ken's voice in the street. He was greeting a long-lost friend with enthusiasm. I wondered who it could be. Then his footsteps again and a ring at the bell. As I came out of the kitchen a tall shadow slipped out of the dining-room. David our Reader, although immersed in the business of the meeting, had picked up the signals going on outside.

'Do you need any help?' he whispered.

'No thank you. It's Ken but he's in a good mood,' I said gratefully. Ken was beaming.

'I've just met yon collie. And he's fine. Wagging his tail and looking well. Made my day. . . .'

'I'm so glad Ken, but I've got to get back to my ironing now. Goodnight.'

'Au revoir, Madame,' he said, and went down the steps again.

There is always someone ready to say, 'Look at all the alcoholics in your churchyard.' We do, frequently. 'Why doesn't the church do something about them?' The speakers are often people who live far away from East London and so they have no idea what the church is doing. Which is plenty.

Not Limehouse Church; it would be crazy if every parish church tried to do something about everything. But the Crypt at Christ Church Spitalfields, the Salvation Army and locally Caplin House, run by the Kenward Trust, are all 'doing something' along with many others.

Most of the men in the churchyard and those who come to our door have no wish to be cured. Alcohol dims your insight from the first drop onwards. But occasionally someone asks for help to get out of this vicious, befuddled circle and we are able to send them to that section of 'the church' which is there to rescue them.

Which leaves me still giving cups of tea and sandwiches to all the others.

'I've just arrived from Glasgow,' said one. 'Never been in this area before. Could you give me some bread and some tea?' He's a big fellow with a scar right down one side of his face. Looks like a Red Indian.

'Really?' I said. 'I've seen you plenty. And don't you remember my husband and me picking you up in the churchyard when you were feeling ill, a few weeks back?'

'Aw Missus, just some bread and some tea,' he said.

He knew it was a fair cop. Telling lies is the alcoholic way of life, and they lack the insight to check themselves when they are speaking to someone who knows the truth.

Sometimes I think they have simply forgotten that they have been before; sometimes they don't credit me with any ability to remember faces. But if the Red Indian fellow thinks I won't remember him and that scar down his face, he has never looked in the mirror!

People like him have not only ruined their own lives, but the lives of their families too. Somewhere up in Glasgow and all those other towns, there are wives and children who have been abused and deserted. Is anyone caring for them? I would rather give bread and tea to them than to the men who have caused their misery. Alcoholics on the doorstep talk smoothly but they are liars, fighters, thieves. They would think nothing of breaking in to steal money from us or from anyone else.

Another man looked ill one day. I had seen that squinting, puckered face so often that I knew it was pain there, not alcohol. Bronchitis perhaps, or TB? Would he like a couple of nights in a bed until he's feeling better? Yes, he says, a bit slurred.

I had already phoned Caplin House while the kettle was boiling and Duncan had said Yes, fine, we can fit him in.

'It's a place where they have people like you who aren't feeling too good,' I explained while he drank his tea. 'You haven't got to stay long or do anything you don't want to. They'll just look after you until you feel a bit better.'

But he never arrived. Couldn't face the thought of being caged in, regimented, documented. Not that they do that at Caplin House but there is no way of getting that across to a man who is suspicious of everyone. He came again, for another summer, perhaps once a month. But I haven't seen him for a long time now. Did he die in hospital, comfortable and cared for at the last, I wonder?

'How are you managing?' I ask another—not an alcoholic—on a day of deep snow.

'Oh I'm fine, thank you Ma'am,' he says with his customary Northern Ireland courtesy. 'I'm sleeping at the Salvation Army at Blackfriars but I don't have the patience to sit there all day like the most of them does. I have to be out.' So he has a weekly warming mug of tea and he's off tramping along the street again, well-clad, as happy as the high king himself.

There are a good many men on the streets but not on the drink, who simply went to pieces after the death of a wife. They did not know how to cope and gradually life disintegrated. They call not so much for a cup of tea as for a kind word and sometimes a clean shirt if we have one.

Occasionally there is a total reversal, unexpected and delightful. Jacob spends a lot of time in the churchyard with his dog. He finds it difficult to read or write and therefore to fill in forms, so he is a squatter in a council flat. He manages to feed himself and his dog and to pass the long days cheerfully. He brought me a bunch of keys he found in the churchyard, and then a blackbird with a damaged wing. One day he came with a sore throat and a cough.

'The doctors round here think I'm one of them drug addicts, just because of me long hair. Can you give me something for me cough?' I poured some glycerine, honey and lemon into a nearly empty bottle of Gee's linctus and gave him a dose on the doorstep, and then the bottle to take home. Next time I met him he said, 'Cor, that medicine was smashing. Got rid of me cough, it did.'

And just before Christmas that year he appeared on the doorstep with a box of chocolates.

'You done a lot for me, giving me that cough medicine,' he said. 'Happy Christmas.'

There are even some borrowers who you know will return the goods. Which is always a pleasant feeling.

There was a concert in our church one evening in aid of the Ragged School Museum. Mick, one of our church members, saw the orchestra into church and then drifted across to the rectory.

'They've all arrived, they've got the spare keys and they know where everything is. There's just one thing,' he said. 'Have you got a pair of pliers you can lend them? There's this geezer wants to tune his harpischord.'

There are exceptions to every rule, even the one about never giving money. We gave Eric a pound on his birthday to buy sausage and chips for two in the chip shop. The pound was a gift from a friend in the country. Eric was delighted. He was a regular caller, tall and strong with flashing eyes and a black beard. He was a schizophrenic and quite capable of throwing dustbins down the streets of Spitalfields when roused. Our front door and letter-box have never been the same since he kicked them.

But in a good mood, no-one could be more affable. 'I saw you on your bicycle today my dear,' he told me once, 'and I was a little concerned for you. The traffic was very heavy.' He once admitted to riding a bike in his younger days, before he lost his sense of balance. 'Wonderful things, bikes,' he said wistfully. Often Mary came with him. Overweight, always good humoured, she tried to calm Eric down if he was in a bad mood.

'Oh come along Eric,' she would say. 'Mrs Idle is very kind. There's no need to get upset.' Gradually he found he could trust us.

'Good evening my dear,' he would say. 'And how are you? And if you could fill the flask with tea I should be so grateful.' He produced a huge flask from his shopping bag and I came in with it and put the kettle on. Sometimes the flask had been broken or stolen, he said, and so he brought a lemonade or whisky bottle instead. Where did he get the next flask from, I often wondered. I was always a little scared of the glass bottle breaking and so I would fish an old sock out of the cleaning cupboard and pull it up over the bottle. There was no sock on it next time Eric called. Did the socks find their way on to his feet?

He always seemed to choose the coldest, foggiest nights to keep me talking at the door; what must it be like to live out in the cold? Like many others, Eric and Mary lived where they could in derelict houses. They would not accept housing because they simply could not cope with officialdom; to them, begging and sleeping rough was simpler. Even at Christmas they stayed outside.

'Crisis at Christmas' organises three or four nights of food and shelter for those who sleep rough. Stores like Marks & Spencer's donate supplies, doctors give their services free and scores of young volunteers work through the days of Christmas for the sake of those who have nothing.

Eric and Mary preferred to carry on as usual, hunting for wood to make a fire. 'It's all very well and kind,' said Eric one year, 'but they're not a very nice type of person that goes there my dear. We're better off on our own than mixing with them.' So they struggled on, finding shelter where they could.

One day Mary came alone. Eric was dead. I brought her into the kitchen, made a pot of tea and wept a few tears for the tramp who once stole a cyclamen plant in its pot off my doorstep.

Eric had staggered into the road a little drunk and been knocked down by a car. He lay in the London Hospital, well cared for until he died.

Mary was being looked after by the nuns at the Crispin Street Free Shelter and looked a lot more spruce and tidy. She had even lost some weight. But she is back on the road now, with a tiny little meek man in tow, a total contrast to Eric.

'Say thank you to Mrs Idle for your nice cuppa tea,' she tells him.

She didn't need to tell Eric.

12

Sorrow in the city

> The days of our age are three score years and ten; and though men be so strong that they come to four score years: yet is their strength then but labour and sorrow; so soon passeth it away and we are gone. . . .
> So teach us to number our days: that we may apply our hearts to wisdom (Ps 90:10, 12).

Dolly was kneeling near the choir pews, a pile of gladioli beside her. I pottered around in the chancel, tidying the two vases up there, and came down the steps to borrow the secateurs. Lovely. She obviously knew just what she was doing. I handed the secateurs back and picked up a duster; it was months since we had had a church funeral and the trestles for the coffin needed a good rub. Then the pews—the church would be full of neighbours.

At last we were done and Dolly's two vases stood by the chancel steps; delicate spikes of coral, rose and peach warming us with their beauty on a cold and sad day. Wagg, who had lived in our street for thirty years, was to be buried today.

'We shall miss him,' said Dolly. 'He was always there. All summer he'd be sitting out there with Laddie, keeping an eye on the church.'

'And before we came,' I reminded her, 'he kept the spare church keys when there was no vicar.'

Dolly thanked me for keeping her company in church.

I thanked her for the flowers and we parted until after lunch.

Playing the organ for a funeral is a great privilege. Not many funerals come to church these days, so it is usually a church member's. It is quite different from playing for a wedding; when two local people want a church wedding it can be a lovely opportunity for the rector to talk to them about God; but sitting up there on the draughty organ seat, I am merely a musician provided by the church.

At a funeral, I am part of the mourning congregation, except that I must keep my eyes dry. For one of my very dear elderly friends we had 'The church's one foundation'—the church full of West Indians singing with all their might. I was fine at the time, but ever since, I've had a job to get through it. There are so many rich hymns one can sing at a Christian's funeral.

One of the hardest funerals was a baby's. When we talked it over, Christopher said, 'I don't think I'll say the usual words when I come in with the coffin; we'll just come in in silence with you playing.'

My heart sank but I didn't say so; he had enough to think about. What was I going to play? I found Golden Bells, which I grew up with, and prayed. Then I marked up some of the old familiar children's hymns, prayed again and put it aside, confident that God would guide me when I was actually up there.

So we had 'When mothers of Salem' and 'I think when I read that sweet story of old' for the voluntary, with others of the same ilk. When the family arrived with the coffin I was playing 'When he cometh, when he cometh to make up his jewels'. Had I done the right thing?

Afterwards over coffee, Iris said to me, 'I did so enjoy those hymns you were playing. I'd forgotten I ever knew them of course, but they seemed so suitable.' I still thank the Lord for that timely reassurance.

At one-thirty on that February day, I was back with an armful of music. It was well-tried—mainly favourite hymns, needing little concentration. Giving of one's best at our local funerals does not consist of high-flown music, brilliantly executed. It lies in watching what is going on and being alert. There is always something different to assimilate. Today it was the arrival of Wagg's family ten minutes ahead of the coffin. 'May we come in?' I heard Em's voice floating up from below me and there they all were, making themselves at home and greeting their friends and neighbours.

The green warning light above the organ flashed twice and I pushed a stop in. 'Tell me the old, old story' was now being played on one diapason stop with the swell box closed. How I wanted them to feel that love around them this afternoon.

'I am the resurrection and the life, saith the Lord, . . .' Christopher was reading, coming slowly up the aisle while the bearers followed him with the coffin. I went on playing until they withdrew.

Leave the motor on, check the . . . whatever is that in the middle of the aisle?

Concentrate, I told myself. Check the registration for 'Abide with me' . . . but it was big and brown and shaggy . . . check the registration, push the sheet music over so that it doesn't flutter down, turn round for the Psalm. Oh, I see now, it's Laddie.

The tears rolled down my cheeks as I joined in the Psalm. How natural and appropriate that the whole family should come to the funeral together, including the faithful old dog. But how very moving it was to see him there.

The neighbours were all there too. George Baker the builder and his men, the families from the houses down the street, and the newcomers—Conservative, SDP and Communist, from the houses opposite.

After it was over, I wondered who would be next, as Winnie and I put the hymn books away. Would it be some elderly parishioner whom we hardly knew, or one of our Christian stalwarts, over seventy?

A few days later, the Head of our church school, Peter Green, went into hospital. He had been at Stepney Greencoat for ten years and the teachers were planning a party in July to mark the occasion. He had been ill for a few months, working as usual for much of the time, and we hoped now for improvement.

I was emptying bins into the dustbin one Friday morning when Christopher came in from school. There was no need to say anything. I took one look at his face, slammed the kitchen door and we clung together. Peter had only a short journey ahead of him. We needed to pray not only for him and his family but for the school, continuing its day to day life without him.

The next Saturday, I went to visit Peter in hospital. He was opening his postcards and letters piled high. His bed-table was a bower of spring flowers.

We talked for five minutes about books and about his family but I could see that he was just keeping exhaustion at bay until I had gone. I kissed him and his smile was as warm as ever; then I ran heedlessly down, down the familiar hospital stairs and got lost in the basement. It was of no importance; I had said goodbye to Peter.

> The Lord is my shepherd:
> therefore can I lack nothing.
> He shall feed me in a green pasture:
> and lead me forth beside the waters of comfort (Ps 23:1, 2).

There came a Wednesday when we recited Psalm 23 at Morning Prayer. Or tried to. I seemed to be crying and waiting for the telephone to ring all day. The parish Bible Study, one of my favourite hours of the week, dragged on pointlessly.

At last it was nine o'clock and we sang a hymn. I moved across to a chair in the corner. Tucked away there, I could cry during the prayers without anyone knowing.

The telephone call came at about ten fifteen. Peter had finished his journey. For him, the glory of heaven.

> . . . in thy presence is fullness of joy: and
> at thy right hand there is pleasure for evermore (Ps 16:12).

For us, one of the livelier boys at school summed it up better than any grown-up could have done. He went into the Head's study and left a note on Peter's chair. It said —

> 'Dear Mr Green. I love you very much.
> I am sorry you died.'

Like hundreds of others, I took time off in the middle of my working day to go to Peter's funeral, that day in May. We were solemn but we also gave thanks for Peter's outrageous sense of humour, as well as praying for his family.

Going straight back into school in the middle of the afternoon, it was difficult to be patient and encouraging with the younger recorder players. I came yawning up the school path at three-thirty, tense and irritable. Tonight we were having an Explorers' picnic; how could I cope?

Halfway up our street I turned left and thundered at Elvey's door. No reply. Occasionally someone was at home; usually I let myself in with the key kindly lent me by the family. Elvey could no longer remember which was Tuesday, so my visits took her by surprise every time. I ran up the stairs calling and she came out of the bedroom.

'Oh darling, you come to see me? You make the day pass quicker. Oh dear heart, I so glad to see you.' Soothed by her endearments, I kissed her soft brown cheek and then took her slowly down the stairs.

'And how are things with you today, dear?' asked Elvey as we sat down together.

'I've just been to a funeral. I'm sad today,' I said, beginning to weep.

She was going blind now, but her kind old eyes had seen a good deal of life and death, and of weeping. So she felt no need to be embarrassed or to hurry me; no need to do anything except pat my shoulder and say,

'There, dear heart. There now, sweetheart, it's all right.' She might have been back in the hot Carribean sunshine, singing a lullaby to one of her sons, or murmuring encouragement to Annie, Mary, Daisy and Jane as they ambled homewards through the orchard to be milked.

After a while, I dried my eyes and opened my Prayer Book at the Collect, Epistle and Gospel for Ascension Day, which was two days away. I lingered over the words and from time to time Elvey nodded or said 'Ah, yes Lord.' I prayed for our families and the church family, and then together we said the Lord's Prayer and 'Lighten our darkness'.

Elvey was tired now. 'Shall I take you back upstairs?' I asked.

'No dear. I let you out, then I go up by myself,' she said. I was always afraid she would trip on the stairs, but I couldn't deny her that bit of independence, so we said goodbye at the kitchen door.

Dear Elvey. I still miss her. When we came to Poplar in 1971, she was an active seventy-three year old, making her views crystal clear on the Church Council. She was often away from home, visiting friends or relatives who were sick; but come winter, she would tuck herself away in her room, running two paraffin stoves and longing for Guyana.

By the time the whole family—son, daughter-in-law and two grandchildren in their twenties—moved to a flat in our street, Elvey was growing frail. She knew that she would never make her journey back to the hot sunshine now.

I would sit and pray with her once a week, always

using the Book of Common Prayer, so that she could savour the old familiar words.

One November afternoon she was weary of illness and longing for heaven. So we held hands and prayed that the Lord would take her soon. By December she was in hospital. But there was a hitch. Her granddaughter had just gone off to Guyana for a long-awaited holiday.

I bumped into the staff nurse one afternoon when I went up to Mile End to visit Elvey.

'We're surprised that she's still here,' said the nurse.

'Well, there's a reason,' I said. 'Her granddaughter is abroad on holiday. Elvey is waiting until she comes back.'

The nurse's eyebrows rose. Maybe she had never heard of the patriarchs of the Old Testament, who calmly settled their affairs and blessed their grandchildren before they departed.

'You could be right,' she said doubtfully. Elvey had been a matriarch all her life and I couldn't see her giving up now. So she paused at the gates of heaven until Anita arrived home on the Saturday afternoon. In the early hours of Sunday morning, Elvey passed through the 'gate of life immortal'.

I cried all through the second hymn and Sue came and put her arm round me.

'I've just heard that a friend of mine has died,' I said. Then I realised she might think I meant a contemporary. So I added triumphantly, 'But she was eighty-five and she's in heaven and I'm very happy really.'

I walked up the street from Elvey's that Tuesday afternoon comforted, almost looking forward to the picnic after all. How does God cope with joy and sorrow simultaneously, I wondered. Can we learn to cope as he does, somehow absorbing the sorrow and treasuring the joy?

The umpteenth heavy shower of the day swept down on me and I prayed for a fine evening, for safety and for all that you need when you take ten-year-olds on an evening picnic.

By seven-thirty, five of us were assembled in the kitchen, warmly clad. Natasha and Mark were chattering away as usual, Nigel was smiling and ready for anything. This was strictly a senior Explorers' outing; the junior members were to have a picnic next week in Victoria Park.

Ruth had brought a bunch of flowers; there was a visit to make before we caught the bus. Just two minutes across the churchyard, we came to Aggie's flat and rang the bell.

'Ready everyone?' Aggie opened the door and we burst into song.

'. . . Happy birthday, dear Aggie,
Happy birthday to you.'

Natasha gave her the flowers and Nigel gave her a card. Aggie didn't say much but her eyes shone. She was eighty.

A hop, skip and jump on to a fifteen bus and we were soon at Aldgate. Down the street past glossy new buildings and crumbling old ones, we came to Colin's flat.

'. . . Happy birthday, dear Colin,
Happy birthday to you.'

Mark gave him a card and I gave him a cake in a tin. Colin knew that Ruth and I were going to arrive with something planned but he had no idea what, in spite of careless whispers among the Explorers. I have never seen him speechless before and I rather enjoyed it. He was twenty-four.

We chattered and skipped and laughed along The Highway and through the gate of the Ivory House. There before us in the cool evening lay St Katharine's

Dock. We wandered along, looking at the boats and the water, a living kaleidoscope of chatter and investigation. Ruth and I were the only ones who had been there before.

Reluctantly, we came up the steps on the west side of Tower Bridge and picnicked near the Tower. When we had finished, the floodlights were on and it looked like a fairy castle.

For the younger ones, a good deal of the beauty of the evening lay in the fact that it was now dark. We strolled back to Colin's flat, still chattering like a barrow-load of monkeys, squashed into his car and just got everyone home by nine-thirty.

I lay awake for a long time that night, unwinding from the day, giving thanks, praying and thinking ahead to Peter's Memorial Service.

We held it on Wednesday, 22nd June, a day of warm, clear sunshine. I rushed through the chores and went down the road to my own school armed with secateurs and a cardboard box. We had arranged that I could raid the garden for all the crimson and gold roses I could find.

'Thanks,' I said in the doorway and took them into church. At ten-thirty, half of Stepney Greencoat school arrived to rehearse and decorate. The teachers had already cleaned the gallery, not normally used, as a loving contribution to the preparations.

I helped with the flowers and then walked up the road with three willing assistants for more armfuls of roses. It was appropriate that they were all in bloom that week, in the garden where Peter used to park his Honda.

We met the school-keeper. 'Have you seen the Parks man?' he said. 'He was going to ask Chris about his staff manning the car park.'

'Seen the Parks man, Dave? There are Parks men all over the churchyard. Every splinter of broken cider bottle is being swept from the asphalt, and every blade of grass is being combed and stood upright.'

People in Salmon Lane stopped us as we walked back with the roses.

'Aren't they lovely? Where are you going with them? Oh, of course, this afternoon, isn't it?'

Over lunch Christopher said a long Grace, praying as we had already done so many times, for the service to be right, a fitting tribute to Peter and entirely honouring to God.

There were so many people taking part, so many suggestions and ideas had been offered, that it had taken a long time to get the balance right. Christopher had been working at it with Helen Chillingworth, the school's acting Head, for the past few weeks.

For once, they both had that odd feeling of confidence that the service would go well—something really special. But Christopher's adrenalin was working overtime on the question 'Would it be the right length?' It must not, must not be too long, and yet people have got to feel they've been to something by the time they walk down the church steps.

I sat at the very back to begin with, on the old pew marked 'Churchwarden.' I was able to greet people I had not seen for months or years, and was on hand if anyone needed me. In the end, I stayed there because there were no other empty seats. People came from all over, local teenagers who had spent their younger days at the school, friends from Cheshire who had been Peter's colleagues on Beach Missions, heads of local schools and department heads from the Inner London Education Authority.

Avril, the school mother who had been chosen to speak for the parents, came and sat beside me for a minute.

'How are you feeling?' I asked. Predictably she said,

'Ooh, my tummy. It's turning over.' Just then, Peter's family slipped quietly into church and sat in their reserved pew near us. Avril took a long look at the back of Wendy's head.

'Well!' she said. 'She's brave to come, isn't she? And if she can do it, I can do it too.' She squeezed my hand and went to her appointed place near the front.

The organ music finished and a clear voice from the gallery began to sing 'Fear not, for I have redeemed thee'. It set the note of quiet trust in God that ran all through the Service.

Friends talked about Peter and showed slides of him. We sang one or two of his favourite songs; I wondered how the people from the Education Office felt, singing 'You can't stop God from loving you'.

But the whole service was a challenge to us to follow the Lord whom Peter followed. So at the end, with a rustling of Service sheets and a clearing of throats, we stood and sang —

'He who would valiant be
'Gainst all disaster,
Let him in constancy
Follow the Master.'

13

Joy in the city

Christ our passover is sacrificed for us:
therefore let us keep the feast (1 Cor 5:7).

I lowered a batch of hot cross buns into the freezer. Do German Baptists eat them, I wondered. And, a quite different question, had I made enough? I rummaged among the bread pudding and pizzas and counted the labels off again. Yes, that made sixty and another six that hadn't got crosses on; that should be enough. The pastry had run out at the end of a busy day; we could have eaten them as buns but I had decided to keep them as spares. We can never be quite sure how many people will turn up for the Parish Walk on Good Friday.

Lent had come and gone quickly, I thought as I tidied the freezer. The dark evenings suddenly disappearing when the clocks went forward. Ash Wednesday succeeded by the Women's World Day of Prayer and Mothering Sunday. The outside world may not be frantic in Lent, the way it is in Advent, but there is still enough to keep the Christians busy.

In many parts of the world, women have very little say in the life of their church and so the Women's World Day of Prayer is a great event in their year. In and around Poplar and Limehouse there are several women's meetings and plenty of opportunities for women to serve God in the family of the church, so the Day is just one more meeting to be planned. But through the years we have enjoyed this annual get-together, with all flavours of church allegiance represented.

One year I was privileged to be the speaker, and as I stood in the pulpit of Trinity Methodist Church, with the sun pouring in on the light oak pews and the upturned faces, I felt moved to make some unscripted remarks.

'Ten years ago,' I said, 'when we came to Poplar, I was pushing a pram. All of you have watched the boys growing up; you all wished us well when we moved to Limehouse. Seeing you here today makes me very happy; I want to thank you for your friendship over the last ten years.' Or something like that. I know I felt very moved as I looked at those elderly ladies, those church workers, those young mothers, and felt I belonged.

Next thing you know, Mothering Sunday is arriving. The Climbers practise a song, the Explorers prepare the prayers and Eddy Stride, Rector of Christ Church Spitalfields, orders quantities of daffodils for his neighbouring clergy friends, from the market.

On the Saturday I am knee-deep in our share of these daffodils, with forsythia from our garden to make the bunches more interesting. Since I wrote the Harvest chapter, the pussy-willows across the road have been grubbed out, along with all the other bushes, to make a formal garden, all tidy and paved. We like a path down to the canal but we are sad to lose our little bit of wilderness.

So no more pussy-willows to go with the daffodils. I make about eighty bunches, put them back in buckets overnight and next day we take them across to church, ready for the Family Service.

Every person, however old, who has a mother in church, is invited to come and receive a bunch. Our boys were always a bit sheepish in their early teens but don't mind so much now.

They have made it clear over the years that there is too much penitence in our usual Order of Service and they are right. A happy 'Thank you God' day can so easily be turned into an 'Aren't children thoughtless; aren't mothers long-suffering' day by boring old grown-ups. We need to watch that.

Next day there are a few visits to make, with bunches of flowers for those who are elderly or ill. Then it is time to think about Easter music; who should sing something special in the Good Friday Family Service or on Easter Day?

And now Holy Week had arrived. I went up the cellar stairs and found Marcus and Hans waiting for me, sounding like Christmas Day in the trenches. Hans had been sent over to England for three weeks, to stay with Kathleen and Rhoda in Canterbury to learn to speak good English. They thought they would be rather dull company for a fourteen-year-old and passed him on to us for the middle week. Where better to learn good English than Limus?

We pulled on our coats and went out into the warm spring sunshine. The blossom on our cherry tree was still tightly curled, waiting for yet one more warm afternoon before shaking itself out. Golden forsythia spilled over the wall; rubbish blew along the street.

Today was Wednesday, a breathing space in the busy week. We were going, at Hans' request, to the Tower of London, Piccadilly Circus and Buckingham, Palace. London Transport has woken up to tourism and the 15 bus goes from the Tower to Oxford Circus, taking in St Paul's Cathedral and Trafalgar Square as a bonus on the way. 'Here they come,' said one bus conductor as the tourists surged on to the bus at the Tower. 'They don't know where they've been and they don't know where they're going.' And sure enough, right on cue, an American woman said, 'Say Elmer, we're on the wrong bus. We should be going the other way.'

We lingered in the sunshine, that Holy Wednesday, while Hans took pictures of Buckingham Palace and then Big Ben. It was the last time we would be lingering anywhere for the next four days.

Maundy Thursday is often ignored these days but the Church of England still keeps it as a solemn festival, the last Communion before Easter.

We treated it like a Saturday, cleaning the shoes, putting the vacuum cleaner round, seeing that everyone had a clean shirt for tomorrow. There were sandwiches to make for Good Friday lunch and the sitting room to be cleared ready for an invasion after the Parish Walk. Oh, and please get the hot cross buns out of the freezer, Jeremy.

Then to church. 'And the disciples were all sitting there with their smelly feet. . . .' said Phil as he preached the sermon. As we came out we carried all the flowers to the back, leaving the church bare.

Good Friday dawned cold and grey, with a bitter wind. We breakfasted on hot cross buns, plenty of them, stoking up for the day ahead. First the Family Service, something straightforward with the children in mind. One year, Dr John and Mrs Audrey Coleman, not long back from Iran and at the centre of world news, came to the service as ordinary visitors. No media, no fuss, just the normal Good Friday service they were hoping for here in England. I looked down from the organ loft and to my delight saw almost all my Explorers there; we had been praying for the Colemans every Sunday since the August day when they had been imprisoned in Tehran. After the service, each of the Explorers was able to shake hands and say 'We prayed for you.'

Today we sang the familiar Good Friday hymns and used prayers from the Book of Common Prayer. There is a favourite one of mine set for this day; it beseeches God lovingly and warmly to 'have mercy on all Jews, Turks, Infidels and Hereticks.' We usually leave those titles out nowadays and say 'Jews, Muslims and Unbelievers' instead. But the sentence which always moves me is 'and so fetch them home blessed Lord to thy flock, that they may be saved among the remnant of the true Israelites, and be made one fold under one shepherd, Jesus Christ our Lord. . . .'

Promptly at eleven-thirty we finished. No coffee; straight home. The day had scarcely begun. I stayed in church to bridge the gap while Christopher went home for a hot drink and a sandwich.

The service to follow was the Three Hours, held from noon to three o'clock. This is a quiet service when we think about the time when our Lord was on the cross for us.

'And it was about the sixth hour,' the Gospel of Luke tells us,' and there was a darkness over all the earth until the ninth hour.' So church members like to come into church for at least a part of that time.

It was warm and quiet at the back of the church; just the hum of the fan heaters and the distant noises of traffic. The books were ready and everything was tidy. I was deep in a book when there was a creak in the gallery above my head. Lyn had arrived. The organ was open, the motor still warm and I had left the music books ready for her. We always share the organist duties at festival times.

A door swung and I heard a bicycle being wheeled in; it was Daniel Pearce who was going to lead the service. His bicycle, like mine at that time, owed nothing to the paint industry—but it did its job.

I stayed for the first hymn and then went over to the rectory for a sandwich. The boys were reading or pottering around quietly. We moved all the downstairs chairs into the sitting-room and put all the hot cross buns into baking tins, ready to be warmed. Then I went back to church and they to their reading.

Today I sat next to Christopher. Most unusual except when we are on holiday. We listened to Daniel and explored with him a little more of the meaning of the Cross. Eight hymns, seven times of prayer, spaced among times of silence and meditation. The service never dragged; rather, it was an oasis in a busy life. People slipped into church or out again during the service and by the end there were about thirty of us, ready to walk through the streets of the parish, to sing and pray and witness in the courtyards among the flats. Once more I returned to the house; this time to whistle up the boys, light the oven for the buns and put the big kettle on.

We locked up and tumbled out into the grey windy afternoon. We had done it all before; it was part of the Good Friday routine now. But we were doing it with sincere hearts and for God and the glory of his Name.

It was all quite new to Hans of course, and here he was, caught up in a surging tide of Idles and swept into the churchyard for some half-understood walk or march. But when we started, he comprehended, good Baptist that he was, and even carried the heavy wooden cross for part of the route.

We gathered round the cross in the first courtyard, among the overflowing rubbish and rolling coke tins. Spicy aromas of curry drifted past. Children watched from doorways. Dogs barked, curtains were lifted, doors were slammed or opened. The roller skate brigade arrived. 'Oh Miss, can we come with you? What are you going to do?' 'We're going to sing about Jesus. Would you like to come and share my hymn sheet?' I knew most of them from school. We sang 'There is a green hill'; Nick lifted up his voice and explained for about three minutes why Jesus 'died that we might be forgiven' and we all said the Lord's Prayer together.

Mick shouldered the cross and we went under the railway bridge, damp with the sullen drip of past rain and fouled by the pigeons who sit on the steel rafters high above.

The next pitch was mine. Different hazards to negotiate here—old mattresses and broken chairs among the smart new cars. We sang 'When I survey the wondrous cross' and then I began.

'Whenever I come round these flats I meet my friends—the friends I've made at school or got to know over the years. We all need friends. . . .' Across the road on the waste ground beside the school annex, a few old bangers were parked. Someone was getting ready for the next Stock Car racing event. He revved the engine. Louder, louder. The group looked at me in sympathy; I knew they were praying for me.

'Jesus is a friend for everyone, you can find all that you've been looking for in him,' I finished.

On then down the street and across Limehouse Causeway to our next stop, where the flats face each other across washing lines and broken prams. Life was noisier and richer here; men under cars, children and dogs playing football, more coke tins rolling in the wind. I waved to children I taught at school, up and up again as they leaned over their balconies. Our numbers were increased by more roller-skaters.

Arlene stood waiting with a brother, two sisters and two friends. All three sisters were learning the recorder at school. Last year Arlene had wanted to tag along with us but her Mum said No. I beckoned her.

'Will your Mum let you come this year?' She nodded, eyes bright at the thought of a hot cross bun at the rectory. She came over and the other five followed, to share our hymn sheets. Six hot cross buns. We sang, proclaimed the Good News and prayed again.

A fine drizzle was falling as we moved to our last pitch, a grassy mound between some of the newer flats at the bottom of our street. Does anyone listen or notice, I asked myself, with the windows closed against the cold? Are we just making an exhibition of ourselves for nothing?

It's a discipline I answered myself, and we're doing it for God. And how do you know nobody notices, anyway?

The roller-skaters got themselves laboriously to the top of the mound. Colin moved back to give them a little more room and murmured something about ' . . . just a little shove? . . .' with a gleam in his eye as he contemplated them sailing down the hill again; but we were already turning our damp hymn sheets over with cold fingers to find 'When I survey' for the second time around.

'Oh Miss, are we coming to your house after?' said Cherene at the end of verse three. The answer was Yes, so I left them singing the last verse and hurried up the street to make tea and take warm buns out of the oven.

It was four o'clock when they all came in. Tim leaned the heavy cross carefully against the wall, Marcus poured orange squash for the younger ones and we all relaxed in the warmth, wrapping our fingers round our teacups. It was a time to linger over second helpings but by five everyone had gone. The boys, in the inimitable way they have when we have all been at full stretch, moved all the chairs back to their respective places before I had even plugged in the vacuum cleaner. We began to unwind after the tensions of the day. I got out the eggs for tea and wondered what sort of a story Arlene was telling her mother about it all.

On Holy Saturday we saw Hans off on the coach to Canterbury and applied ourselves to Easter breakfast. Butter, marmalade, bread and eggs for forty four people.

It all began in 1973 when Christopher was Priest-in-charge of St Matthias church in Poplar. Something called 'Spree 73' suggested that people might like to have their first Holy Communion of Easter Day out in the open, at sunrise. Sunrise? Well . . . perhaps a little after. . . . Our neighbour, Eddy Stride at Spitalfields, wanted to use the suggestion but their churchyard was not available that year. Doubtless his good friend Christopher Idle would fall in with the idea and welcome them all to the grassy plot surrounding St Matthias church.

So that year and ever since, we have shared the 'Sunrise service' with Christ Church, taking it in turns to be the hosts. Sometimes there has been snow on the ground: one year they had to have the service inside, emerging for the last hymn into the snow—to find the sun shining.

Nowadays, of course, we have the crypt for serving breakfast. But my most vivid memory is of serving it in the house that year when there were forty four takers. On Easter Eve we gathered up armfuls of china and cutlery from the church gallery, two big teapots and a box of eggcups. We tidied the house again and moved the bedroom tables downstairs. Jeremy and Marcus loaded up the trolley and laid the breakfast places—sixteen in the dining room, eighteen (I can't think how) in the sitting-room, ten in the hall. The first year we had Easter breakfast, I was daft enough to move the kitchen table into the hall, leaving myself without enough surface to put things on. Too late, I realised that I had done what one politician described as 'sawing off your own legs at the start of a race.' Each year we managed better, and perhaps appeared less flustered. It gave us a lot of pleasure, that last time, when one of the visitors said, 'Thanks for the breakfast, you made it look easy.'

> Christ is risen from the dead: and become the first-fruits of them that slept.
> For since by man came death: by man came also the resurrection of the dead.
> For as in Adam all die: even so in Christ shall all be made alive (1 Cor 15:20).

On Easter Day we were awake at dawn. Before seven o'clock I had slipped out into the cool morning with a white cloth for the Communion Table. Along the cobbled passage I went, up the wide west steps. Our great west doors stood open for the passage of chairs, benches and a table, to be set up on the green slope near the back-garden walls of our street. It is flatter to the north, in front of the church on the wide expanse of grass under the plane trees. But the passing traffic would have drowned our voices.

Back in the house I woke Jonathan and we had a

leisurely breakfast together. Ever since the snowy Easter in Poplar when he made sixty pieces of toast and didn't get one himself, he has been the breakfast specialist.

The pleasure of family cards and Easter eggs would have to wait until we were all together at lunch-time. We put milk in every jug we possessed and butter in the few remaining dishes. I made porridge in our biggest saucepan while Jonathan finished laying the tables. Stir porridge with left hand, load toaster with right.

The other three came downstairs carrying their bedroom chairs and set to work. Timothy arranged the seating—we had borrowed some chairs from the church. Jeremy fetched in from the back doorstep all the milk we had no room for in the fridge. Marcus fed the cat and helped with last-minute washing up. Then Jeremy went up to his bedroom again, to watch the churchyard from his window.

'They've finished,' he called after a short vigil.

'They're carrying their chairs back into church.'

'Let 'em come,' said Jonathan, 'we're ready for 'em.'

Cool churchyard and empty stomachs do not tempt the congregation to linger and chat after the service. I poured twenty cups of tea before the doorbell rang, so that people could warm up a little before breakfast began.

Suddenly the house was full of people talking, greeting me, scraping their chairs, appreciating the warm house. More tea to pour and in go the eggs.

Last to arrive were the two rectors, Eddy and Christopher. Somehow there were forty-four people sitting down to breakfast. We sang Grace and passed hot bowls of porridge along the tables.

When the boiled eggs had been served, Jonathan and I had a minute to sit down and drink a cup of tea with our guests. There was a busy day ahead for all of us but there was joy at our assorted tables.

'The Lord is risen. He is risen indeed. Alleluia.'